MEXICO CITY

CITYSCOPES: a unique overview of a city's past as well as a focused eye on its present. Written by authors with intimate knowledge of the cities, each book provides a historical account with essays on the city today. Together these offer fascinating vignettes on the quintessential and the quirky, the old and the new. Illustrated throughout with compelling historical images as well as contemporary photos, these are essential cultural companions to the world's greatest cities.

Titles in the series:

Beijing Linda Jaivin

Berlin Joseph Pearson

Buenos Aires Jason Wilson

Chicago: From Vision to Metropolis Whet Moser

Mexico City: Cradle of Empires Nick Caistor

New York Elizabeth L. Bradley

Paris Adam Roberts

Prague: Crossroads of Europe Derek Sayer

San Francisco: Instant City, Promised Land Michael Johns

CITYSCOPES

Mexico City

Cradle of Empires

Nick Caistor

REAKTION BOOKS

To Jack, Luca, Dylan and *la pequeña*, travellers of the future.

Published by Reaktion Books Ltd
Unit 32, Waterside
44–48 Wharf Road
London N1 7UX, UK

www.reaktionbooks.co.uk

First published 2019
Copyright © Nick Caistor 2019

Printed and bound in China by 1010 Printing International Ltd

A catalogue record for this book is available from the British Library
ISBN 978 1 78914 073 6

OPENING IMAGES p. 6: Pedestrians behind the cathedral; p. 7: Diners in the historic House
of Tiles; p. 8 (top): Aztec serpent sculpture in the Templo Mayor, (bottom) Colourful house
in Coyoacán; p. 9: Saturday dancing at La Ciudadela; p. 10: The Torre Latinoamericana; p. 11:
Massive sculpture on the Monument to the Revolution; p. 12: (top): Day of the Dead parade,
(bottom) The vast La Merced market; p. 13 (top): Traditional tortilla maker, (bottom) One
of the many colourful Mexico City markets; p. 14 (top): Lucha libre in the Zocalo, (bottom)
Football fans at a cup final; p. 15: Sunday cycling on Reforma Avenue

Contents

Popocatépetl looming over Mexico City on a rare clear day.

Prologue

Mexico City has always been a seat of empire. In its grandiose pretentions and sheer swagger, it gives the impression of power exercised over great distances. And yet this power has frequently been contested, lending the city and its inhabitants a tough, battle-hardened character – on the one hand, arrogance and condescension; on the other, generosity and magnanimity. Warring armies have clashed repeatedly here in the capital, and often destroyed its architectural heritage, but over the centuries the interludes of peace have seen the city grow with increasing splendour and energy. Always, though, there is also the feeling that there is a thin line in Mexico City between life and death.

The city lies in the shadow of volcanoes; it is built on the beds of several ancient lakes, and has often suffered floods and disruption as parts of the centre have sunk further and further into the soft earth. Even more devastating have been the earthquakes that regularly threaten the city's people and its fabric. The most devastating of these, in 1985, caused the deaths of as many as 10,000 people, the collapse of many thousands of buildings and such a political upheaval that it was one of the main factors behind the crumbling of the party that had ruled Mexico since the late 1920s. On the very same day 32 years later, another huge earthquake shook the city centre, leading to hundreds of deaths and even more destruction.

Man-made destruction has also wreaked its damage, from the fire and carnage wrought by the Spaniards in their sixteenth-century conquest, to the ravages of the revolution that was often fought out on the streets of the capital from 1910 to 1920, and more recent outrages such as the massacre of students in the Plaza de las Tres Culturas in Tlatelolco just before the Olympic Games in 1968.

Perhaps it is precisely this sense of danger that gives life in the Mexican capital its special edge. The city continues to act as a powerful magnet for Mexican migrants from the countryside, who come in search of brighter prospects. By the second half of the twentieth century, this influx had turned it into a sprawling metropolis of more than 20 million inhabitants. When the Spaniards arrived five centuries ago, the clear air at altitudes of more than 2,000 metres (6,500 ft) in the central valley of Mexico led them to name it 'the most transparent region'. But the fact that it lies at the centre of a natural bowl surrounded by snow-topped mountains has meant that air pollution has kept step with the expanding population. On days in late winter and early spring (from January to March or April in this region) when there is no wind, smog can fill the air and make it hard to breathe. More than 3.5 million vehicles clog the city's main streets, and the surrounding industries add to the toxic mix.

And yet life in the Mexican capital can be carefree and intoxicating. Every street seems to be bursting with colour, from the stalls of the vendors to the squares and markets that have not yet been replaced by anonymous shopping centres. Young people are everywhere, determined to enjoy themselves, and they bring life to every corner. The city continues to be the nation's hub for writers, painters, musicians and film-makers – anyone who wishes to make their way in Mexico in the arts, business or politics. Mexicans love to eat and drink, and so the city is bursting with cafés, restaurants and bars, from the louchest cantinas to the smartest venues offering postmodern Mexican and international cuisine. Breakfasts are social occasions that can go on for hours, to be followed by even longer late lunches that take you through the afternoon until it's time for dinner.

The past presses in on all sides: from the churches, the museums, the historic buildings and the faces of the people who were once proudly baptized as the 'bronze race' for the mixture of peoples and ethnicities they represent. Although nearly all Mexicans speak

Spanish – and the Spanish of Mexico is rich in its own special vocabulary, insults and inventiveness – the capital is also the place to hear many of the indigenous languages that still thrive throughout the nation. As in many countries, those Mexicans living outside the capital are both scornful and envious of its inhabitants, calling them *chilangos* or *defeños* (from the official title of the city as the Distrito Federal) and seeing them as arrogant and unfriendly.

The city has grown chaotically over the centuries. The Aztec settlement of Tenochtitlán was built on an island in the middle of one of the old lakes, Lake Texcoco, and was linked to the mainland by three giant causeways. The Spaniards made this the heart of their city as well, and, as they did throughout their empire, imposed a chequerboard structure on the capital of what they termed 'New Spain'. For three centuries, their North American colony stretched from California in the north to Guatemala in the south, all of it governed from the Mexican capital. Although many kilometres from both the Pacific and Atlantic coasts, its pull as the centre of a previous empire was sufficiently strong to dissuade the Spaniards from re-establishing the capital anywhere else. Colonial trade was based there, and all the riches of silver, gold and agriculture produced in the often-distant reaches of the country accumulated in the capital. Government offices, banking and finance, as well as many other industries, were clustered in Mexico City.

When the Spaniards (or *gachupines* as they were scornfully dubbed by the Mexicans) were kicked out at the start of the nineteenth century, the capital saw further growth as Mexico was opened up to the rest of the world. The French and British brought wealth to the growing metropolis, which even saw a brief new empire created, only for it to be swept away after less than two years, and a republic proclaimed in its place. In the aftermath of this struggle, the stability brought about by Porfirio Díaz in the last decades of the century led to the development of roads and railways. These increasingly linked Mexico City to the rest of the country, expanding its influence and helping to bring in more peasants from the often bitterly poor countryside to work in the new factories being set up haphazardly in the capital.

Upmarket shopping centre in Nuevo Polanco.

This pre-eminent position was only emphasized further during the years of revolution from 1910 to the 1920s. While local *caudillos* in the countryside fought for control, hundreds of thousands of peasants sought refuge in the capital. This process continued from the 1930s to the 1950s, by which time the population of the capital had reached 8 million, with many millions more in the surrounding areas that are part of the State of Mexico rather than the capital itself.

Writers have often seen the 1985 earthquake as the coming of the apocalypse for the Mexican capital. The destruction and chaos it caused have brought about serious efforts to plan for growth and to rationalize the city's political and social structures. In 1997 a city mayor, Cuauhtémoc Cárdenas, was elected for the first time, and he was given powers to further plan and develop the city. In 2016 another step was taken when the capital became an autonomous

The corner of Paseo de la Reforma, with the new 'Caballito' sculpture.

region with powers to elect its own public officials, and the city's *delegaciones*, or boroughs, were also granted greater autonomy.

Like many other vibrant cities, there are always new districts that are being built or rediscovered in Mexico City, whether it be the reconstruction of the historic centre or ambitious schemes such as Nuevo Polanco, which see new museums, skyscraper offices and shopping centres rise up almost overnight. However, alongside them there are neighbourhoods where centuries-old traditions still appear to be the norm, especially in the outer suburbs. These are not administratively part of the capital, even though there is little physical distinction between the city and its outlying districts. It is here that most of the recent population growth has been concentrated, and also where extreme poverty and ostentatious wealth jostle each other.

The challenges facing Mexico City in the twenty-first century are enormous. There are centuries-old problems, such as how to drain water and how to maintain the stability of the city's structures on the sandy volcanic soil. These combine with more recent issues, like the chaos of the traffic and the stifling pollution or the need to build a new airport that is safer and more spacious than the current one, which has now been engulfed by the city. The Mexican capital is far from being the utopian city imagined by the Spaniards in the early sixteenth century, and yet it continues to offer any visitor not only glimpses of past grandeur, but the wealth of fascinating culture available in Mexico today.

HISTORY

The Aztecs arriving at the site of Tenochtitlán.

1 The Founding of Tenochtitlán

Ponder this, eagle and jaguar knights,
Though you are carved in jade, you will break;
Though you are made of gold, you will crack;
Even though you are a quetzal feather, you will wither.
We are not forever on this earth;
Only for a time are we here.
Nezahualcoyotl, the poet-ruler of the Acolhua
people living on the shores of Lake Texcoco
in the mid-fifteenth century

Before the coming of the Spaniards in the sixteenth century, before the arrival of the Mexica, or Aztecs, in the fourteenth century, a thriving population already lived in and around the five lakes to be found at the centre of the Valley of Mexico. Situated at over 2,000 metres (6,500 ft) above sea level, and more or less midway between the Pacific and Atlantic coasts, the valley is a vast hollow encircled by mountains, volcanoes and once dense forests. Millions of years ago, a volcanic eruption is thought to have thrown up mountains that cut off the rivers that flowed through the valley from their outlet to the Pacific Ocean, creating an enclosed natural system with both salt- and freshwater lakes. This valley was home to abundant wildlife and attracted early groups of hunter-gatherers. They settled around the lakes and on islands within them, living via fishing and agriculture. Mexican historians date the first settlements in the Valley of Mexico to more than 20,000 years ago.

Some 50 kilometres (30 mi.) outside today's capital city, it has been estimated that between 25,000 and as many as 100,000 people lived in and around Teotihuacán (the Place of the Gods) before it was abandoned in the seventh or eighth century after what appears to have been a devastating fire. Nowadays it is one of the main tourist attractions to the northeast of Mexico City, with massive pyramids and temples at the centre of a site covering more than 20 square kilometres (7½ sq. mi.). Monumental buildings line the central axis of the Avenue of the Dead, perhaps the most spectacular of them being the Temple of Quetzalcoatl. This low pyramid has six levels, all decorated with stone heads that alternately show the Fire Serpent and the Plumed Serpent. But it is the huge Pyramid of the Sun that most tourists come to visit. This pyramid is some 70 metres (230 ft) high and 225 metres (740 ft) long, and is thought to have been built around the first century AD. Close by is the Pyramid of the Moon, with murals showing the Paradise of Tlaloc, the rain god, and others depicting the traditional ball game known as *ollamalitzli*, and human sacrifice.

As with many of the early civilizations of Mexico, the cause of the decline and fall of Teotihuacán remains unclear. Beyond the grandiose monuments, little is known of the lives and beliefs of its inhabitants. Following the collapse of the city, the Valley of Mexico saw the spread of much smaller centres of habitation, with many different groups coexisting or fighting for dominance.

It was not until several centuries later that the Aztecs came to exert their control over many of these existing groups. According to legend, the Aztecs were a nomadic people who in the thirteenth century migrated from their home of Aztlán (the Place of Herons), in the northwest of Mexico, to the Valley of Mexico. They were said to have followed a prophecy by their war god, Huitzilopochtli, that they should migrate towards a spot where they would find an eagle devouring a serpent on a nopal cactus rising from a rock (the image now in the centre of the red, white and green Mexican flag). The place they arrived at is thought to have been on the hill of Chapultepec (Hill of Grasshoppers). Freshwater springs nearby and the abundance of wildlife led the wandering Aztecs to settle there. This is said to have taken place in 1325, which is traditionally accepted as the date for the foundation of the Aztec capital of Tenochtitlán.

Cultivating maguey, from a map of Tenochtitlán, c. 1550.

Their settlement grew over the following generations, and by the fifteenth century the Aztecs began to expand, thanks mainly to their conquest of neighbouring indigenous groups. In around 1430 their armies defeated their main rivals, the Tepanecs, and they soon established an empire that extended far beyond the confines of the Valley of Mexico. With conquest came trade, including gold, silver, jade and other precious goods that underlined the splendour of Aztec rule. Over the next ninety years, the Aztecs expanded Tenochtitlán, on an island on the middle of Lake Texcoco, the largest of the interconnected lakes in the centre of the valley. The Aztec capital is thought to have contained anywhere between 100,000 and 250,000 inhabitants. To help feed this population living in the lakes and marshes, the ingenious system of *chinampas* was developed. These were small floating islands of mud and vegetation that provided extremely rich soil for cultivating vegetables and fruits. The diet of the Aztecs was chiefly composed of the maize, squashes, beans and chillies produced by this system, as well as the abundant fish from the lakes and game that roamed in the hills. Archaeologists have also found evidence that they ate snakes, iguanas, grasshoppers and other insects, worms, and the algae growing on the surface of the waters. They used canoes to get around the lakes, and the canals they created between the artificial islands allowed the inhabitants to transport themselves and their goods throughout the city with ease.

Tenochtitlán was connected to the lakeshore by three huge earthen causeways, which radiated out from the imperial palace at the heart of the city. A wall surrounded the central religious precinct, with basalt figures of jaguars at its base. Inside this wall stood many stone temples, built with pyramids on their summits that are said to have been a representation of the power of the volcanoes visible on the horizon. The different parts of the Aztec city were well defined, with straight roads and canals separating the different districts, which were divided according to the activities that took place there.

Although the Aztec rulers lived in magnificent palaces and the priests had no less splendid temples, most of the population of Tenochtitlán lived in wattle and daub huts with grass roofs. They slept on mats, kept a fire in the middle of the room and often decorated the land outside with flowers. They reared *guacalotes*, or turkeys; dogs and rabbits, which were frequently used to supplement their diet; and parrots and macaws for their feathers, which were used in cloaks and headdresses. In his book *Daily Life of the Aztecs*, the French ethnologist Jacques Soustelle provided a poetic description of how

Cultivating maguey. An Aztec woman blows maize before putting it into the pot so it will not 'fear' the fire.

he imagined the day beginning for these ordinary inhabitants of the Aztec capital:

> With their wicker fans the women blow on the fire that smoulders between the hearth-stones, and then, kneeling before the *metlatl* of volcanic stone they begin grinding the maize. The work of the day begins with this dull rumble of the grinder: it has begun like this for thousands of years. A little later comes the rhythmic slapping of the women gently flattening the maize-dough between their hands to make the pancake-like tortillas or *tlaxcalli.*

In addition to this everyday routine, a large part of life was devoted to keeping the more than two hundred deities in the Aztec pantheon happy, or at least to appeasing their wrath and maintaining stability on earth. In a land plagued by earthquakes and volcanic eruptions, the destructive power of the gods constantly seemed a threat. Perhaps this is why Aztec religious ceremonies often involved human sacrifice, especially to the two main gods, Huitzilopochtli, the god of war, and Tlaloc, the god of rain and agriculture. Usually the victims were prisoners captured during wars with neighbouring groups, although it seems that slaves and even Aztec children were also offered for sacrifice. Early in the sixteenth century one of the Spanish conquerors, Andrés de Tapia, calculated that there had been around 136,000 victims sacrificed at the Templo Mayor (Great Temple). As recently as 2017, archaeologists found proof that de Tapia's story was not entirely invented, when they discovered a circular tower close to the temple encrusted with almost seven hundred skulls of men, women and children.

By the time the Spaniards arrived, the emperor of the Aztecs was Moctezuma II (the great-grandson of the 'irascible prince' Moctezuma I). As well as ruling over Tenochtitlán and the neighbouring lakeside towns, he controlled territory and exacted tributes as far away as what is now the Gulf of Mexico in the east. Although his rule appeared solid, and Aztec society built on firm foundations, there were disturbing portents that he could not ignore. The Aztec

The excavated Aztec Templo Mayor in the city centre.

TEMPLO MAYOR

At the heart of the Aztec capital of Tenochtitlán stood the Templo Mayor, or Great Temple. This is said to have been built on the spot where the Aztecs first saw the eagle devouring a serpent that was the sign for them to found their city. The temple is a stone representation of Coatepetl, the 'Hill of Serpents', the mythic birthplace of the Aztec world.

It was here that Huitzilopochtli, the god of war, defeated the moon goddess, Coyolxauhqui, whose dismembered body lay at the foot of the hill. Coatepetl was located at the navel of the Aztec world. The wide platform on which the twin temples were raised is said to represent the earth. Above it are thirteen tiers which symbolize the Aztecs' thirteen heavens, while beneath it are nine levels that descend to Mictlan, where the dead reside.

The Templo Mayor was levelled in the final assault by Cortés in 1521. For more than four and a half centuries, it survived only in the written records of the conquerors and the painted codices of the defeated. Then, in February 1978, workers laying new electrical cables behind the cathedral in the northern corner of the Zócalo uncovered the edge of a round stone 3 metres (10 ft) in diameter. When the site was explored by archaeologists, the disc was revealed to be the image of the shattered body of Coyolxauhqui. Over the next four years the dig was extended. The terraces were carefully uncovered, and in them were found more than 6,000 statues, other ritual objects and sculptures and figures from as far distant as Oaxaca and the Gulf Coast.

Today the remains of the temple are visible from metal walkways, offering views of the terraces and the upper levels. A well-designed museum containing the finds from the archaeological digs is located above and behind the remains. Its centrepiece is the Coyolxauhqui stone, which can be seen on the same level and also from above, giving some idea of how it must have looked many centuries ago.

Artist's impression of the ceremonial centre of Tenochtitlán.

calendar was based on four different epochs, each represented by a different sun. But now, according to priestly calculations, the Aztecs were living in a fifth era, which was predicted to end in catastrophe, a twilight of the gods more terrible than Wagner's.

Early in the 1500s, Moctezuma and his people began to receive reports of strange newcomers who had arrived on the coast to the east. These reports coincided with the passage of comets, storms and floods that seemed to presage disaster. Then in 1518 more definite news arrived (as recorded by Moctezuma II's grandson, the historian Tezozomoc) that 'two towers had been seen moving about on the sea off the coast'. Moreover, 'the skins of these people are white, much more so than our skins are. All of them have long beards and hair down to their ears'. Moctezuma sent emissaries to exchange gifts with the newcomers, who then departed, promising to return.

A year later, in 1519, Cortés and his men landed. Moctezuma and his people were now faced with new and terrifying wonders. The strangers rode horses, beasts not previously known in the Americas. They carried their goods on wheeled carts – the wheel too was unknown to the indigenous populations. Other wheeled machines

– the Spaniards' cannons – fired balls that could destroy trees and the earth all around them, giving off smoke and a foul stench. Cortés was to write back to the Emperor Charles v in 1520 that Moctezuma accepted his authority because in their history the Aztecs had previously been ruled by Quetzalcoatl, a lord who had one day vanished, promising to return. In 1550 the Spanish historian Juan Ginés de Sepulveda wrote that the ruler of the Aztecs fully accepted that 'the Spanish soldier had arrived with the authority and aid of the gods to reclaim the rights of the ancient monarchy'.

According to Cortés, the Aztec emperor then told him:

We have always held that those who descended from him would come and conquer this land and take us as their vassals. So because of the place from which you claim to come, namely from where the sun rises, and the things you tell us of the great lord or king who sent you here, we believe and are certain that he is our natural lord.

This was of course special pleading by the leader of the invading army. Moctezuma appears to have been disturbed by the priestly prophecies of the end of an era, and to have been thrown into confusion by the sheer incongruous appearance of the Spaniards. He thus hesitated over going to war with the newcomers. As Hugh Thomas has written in his monumental *The Conquest of Mexico*: 'According to his code, he could not prepare for war against the Castilians, since that implied all kinds of rituals, embassies, warnings to submit, presents of clubs and shields to the enemy, formal organization and enlistment of soldiers.'

While he hesitated, in August 1519 Cortés and his three hundred or so men marched resolutely 320 kilometres (200 mi.) up from the coast towards the capital. Along the way, they made allies with many peoples who were tired of paying tribute to Moctezuma and gladly joined Cortés in his confrontation with the Aztecs. Within two years of the arrival of these terrifying foreigners, by mid-1521, Moctezuma ii was dead, many of his people were killed with him and the once mighty city of Tenochtitlán was razed to the ground.

The city of Tenochtitlán at the time of the Spanish conquest.

2 The Spanish Conquest

In early 1519, Hernán Cortés, who since 1511 had been living on Cuba, one of the earliest Spanish strongholds in the New World, left the island with some five hundred men aboard six ships, heading west. Their intention was to explore the coastline of what is modern-day Mexico, discovered for Europeans by Spanish sailors some ten years earlier, and to see how far inland they could progress. They were to take possession of any new territory they found in the name of Charles v, the Emperor of Spain, and convert the peoples they encountered to Christianity – whether they liked it or not.

Cortés and his men landed on the eastern coast of mainland Mexico in February 1519. At first they were welcomed by the indigenous peoples they met, but they soon came up against resistance once the local populations realized they were not gods but human beings like them, however terrifying their horses and weaponry. Nevertheless, the conquistadores pressed on over the next few months across the 240 kilometres (150 mi.) or so separating them from what they had heard was the magnificent capital of the Aztec race, the most powerful in the region. Somewhat to their surprise, the warriors of the other tribes seemed keen to join them if there was to be a fight against the Aztecs, to whom they had paid tribute for many years.

The first meeting with Moctezuma II, the ruler of the Aztec capital Tenochtitlán, was polite. The Spaniards were ceremoniously welcomed into the city along the causeway that led out across the lakes to the south. Cortés gave the Aztec emperor a collar of pearls; Moctezuma welcomed the Spanish leader and his men with great courtesy, and lodged them in his dead father's palace in the centre of the city.

This tale is well known because this is the beginning of the written record the Spaniards kept of the conquest of Mexico. Not only did Cortés, like Columbus before him, send back long, detailed descriptions of his adventures and actions to the Spanish monarch, but some members of his army, notably Bernal Díaz del Castillo, offered eyewitness accounts of the events they lived through. Writing in old age, safely back in Spain, Bernal Díaz provides us with the original Spanish account of what the conquistadores saw when they first glimpsed the mighty Tenochtitlán, in *Historia verdadera de la Nueva España*:

> We arrived at a broad causeway and continued our march towards Iztapalapa, and when we saw so many cities and villages built in the water and other great towns on dry land and that straight and level causeway leading towards Mexico, we were amazed and said it was like the enchantments they tell of in the legend of Amadis, on account of the great towers and temples and buildings rising from the water, and all built of masonry. And some of our soldiers even asked whether the things that we saw were not a dream.

The Franciscan friar Aguilar, who interpreted for Cortés, was equally impressed with the palace of Axayácatl in the heart of Tenochtitlán, where the Spaniards were housed as respected guests in November 1519:

> It was a wonder to behold. There were innumerable rooms inside, antechambers, splendid halls, mattresses of large cloaks, pillows of leather and tree fibre, good eiderdowns, and admirable white fur robes, in addition to well-made wooden seats.

Soon afterwards, according to one of the letters Cortés sent back to his own emperor, the Aztec ruler explicitly recognized the distant monarch as his lord and master. This was because according

Portrait of Hernán Cortés by an unknown artist, probably a 19th-century copy.

to Aztec prophecies, a new lord was to come from the east and ensure the continued existence of the Aztecs after one of the most dangerous junctures in their cyclical calendar. Cortés was naturally pleased that Moctezuma should yield to him and his tiny force without a struggle. Moctezuma, meanwhile, by all accounts seems to have had a genuine admiration for this strange being who had appeared from nowhere, bringing with him powerful, unknown weapons, swords of steel, armour and horses, previously unseen on the American continent.

Within a few days, however, relations had soured. Some of the Spanish captains became apprehensive when they realized they were surrounded by many thousands of Aztecs whose state of mind was largely a blank to them. They talked of being trapped in a 'spider's web'. Surrounded by perhaps 250,000 people who could turn against him at any moment, Cortés forced Moctezuma to leave his palace and join the Spaniards in their quarters. At the same time, he was careful to maintain the outward show that his noble prisoner was still the lord of the Aztecs. 'He would allow Moctezuma to continue to govern his empire. But he, Cortés, would govern Moctezuma,' as the historian Hugh Thomas put it.

This situation lasted for several months, until Cortés went a step further and insisted that Moctezuma agreed not only to become a vassal of the Spanish emperor, but to convert to the Christian faith. Soon afterwards, Cortés and some of his men climbed to the top of the Templo Mayor and ordered the removal or destruction of the pagan idols displayed there. They were to be replaced with images of the Virgin Mary and St Christopher, and once the blood of human sacrifice had been cleaned away, the site was to be turned into a church.

At this point, Cortés was forced to leave Tenochtitlán to deal with a challenge from another Spanish commander sent by the governor of Cuba to rein him in. In his absence, Moctezuma apparently began stirring up his people to rebel against the Spanish garrison, which they attacked repeatedly and came close to overrunning.

As soon as he heard this news, Cortés rushed back to Tenochtitlán. He accused the Aztec ruler of betraying him and refused to meet the man he now referred to as a 'treacherous dog'. The attacks on the Spaniards intensified, led by members of Moctezuma's family. In an attempt to calm the situation, Cortés is said to have forced Moctezuma to go up onto the roof of the Axayácatl Palace and speak to his followers. By now, however, many of the Aztecs no longer accepted his position of authority and they threw a barrage of stones at him.

According to the version written by the Spanish chroniclers, at least three of these stones hit Moctezuma and caused his death the following day. But the Mexican account of his death is very different: they maintain that he was killed by the Spaniards. An exhibition of codices on show at Mexico City's National Museum of Anthropology in 2014 appeared to confirm this. The evidence for this is provided by the Codex Moctezuma, which was on display for the first time since its recent restoration. The codex is a history of the Tenochtitlán region from approximately 1483 to after the Spanish conquest in 1523. One image shows Cortés forcing the bound Moctezuma to the roof of a pyramid, where he is shown talking to his people. But it is the small illustration next to this that has caused a fresh debate over just how Moctezuma died. It depicts a very Spanish-looking steel blade being thrust into the Aztec leader's side. Did the Spaniards kill him, and then blame his death on his own people so as to sow confusion? According to another Aztec codex, Moctezuma's body was laid on a funeral pyre and incinerated. 'Flames roared up. Moctezuma's body lay sizzling and it smelled foul as it burned,' the chronicle tells us.

The reaction to Moctezuma's violent death led the Spaniards to reassess their position. They were in an enemy capital, surrounded by thousands of warriors, and had just killed their emperor, whom the Aztecs regarded as a deity. Cortés decided that for once discretion was the better part of valour. At midnight on 1 July 1520 he ordered the withdrawal of his army along the causeway leading west across the lake towards Tacuba. As they began the crossing, the Spaniards came under attack from thousands of hostile Aztecs in canoes, and discovered that the causeway had been cut, blocking their retreat. By the time this *Noche triste*, or 'Night of Sorrows', was over, the Spaniards had lost several hundred men and much of the huge quantity of gold they had accumulated. The remnants of the army finally managed to straggle to the mainland. Cortés and his depleted forces regrouped as best they could in the town of Tlaxcala, where the indigenous people were still friendly towards them.

While Cortés was pondering how to regain his foothold in Tenochtitlán, a new young emperor was chosen to lead the Aztec nation. He was Cuauhtémoc (Falling Eagle), who set about rebuilding the fortifications of Tenochtitlán while Cortés and his men attempted to subdue or win over the territory and peoples around the lakes. By June 1521 the conquistadors had returned to besiege the capital, constantly probing its defences. Cuauhtémoc and almost the entire population fought back so fiercely that Cortés gave orders for the city's temples, houses and palaces to be destroyed whenever

Hernán Cortés and La Malinche with Moctezuma II.

LA MALINCHE

To carry out his conquest, Hernán Cortés needed the peoples he met to understand the power and glory not only of the Spanish Empire under Charles v, but of the Christian god in whose name he was acting. To achieve this, he relied on interpreters who spoke the local languages as well as Castilian.

One of these was Friar Gerónimo de Aguilar, a priest who had been shipwrecked in the Yucatán in 1511 and by the time of his rescue by Cortés spoke one of the Mayan languages. The other interpreter, who was even more important, was a Nahua woman called Malinalli. She was one of a group of twenty women slaves given to the Spaniards when they landed on the Gulf Coast of Mexico in 1519. At first the verbal exchanges between the new arrivals and the local peoples had to pass between her and Friar Aguilar. Soon, however, she learned enough Spanish to be able to translate directly from the Mexica language. Not only this, but she became Cortés's mistress, and is said to have been the first indigenous woman who converted to Christianity, taking the name Marina.

Marina accompanied Cortés throughout the conquest of Tenochtitlán, withdrawing with him and his army during the 'Night of Sorrows', and returning triumphantly with them in 1521. By 1522 she was installed in her own house in the village of Coyoacán, where she gave birth to a son by Cortés, christened Martín.

In Mexico, however, Marina has another name: La Malinche. As such, she is a more controversial figure. In his most famous work, *The Labyrinth of Solitude*, the twentieth-century poet and essayist Octavio Paz sees La Malinche as the symbol of the way the Mexican peoples were not only vanquished but raped by the Spanish conquerors. Her mixed-race son, Martín, is seen as the first *mestizo*, an uneasy mix of two clashing cultures. As such, Paz argues, Mexicans' attitude towards themselves has often been one of a sense of shame at being the product of this unequal union. This is most often heard in the expression '*hijo de la chingada*', the bastard offspring not at home in either culture.

Since Paz's day, Mexican feminist writers have fought against this interpretation, casting La Malinche/Marina in a much more positive light.

the opportunity arose. As one of the conquerors claimed at the time: 'in order to win the city, it was necessary to demolish it.' The Aztec resistance lasted for several months, until finally Cuauhtémoc himself was captured and brought before the triumphant Spanish commander. In an eloquent speech, recounted by the native historian Ixtlilxochitl, Cuauhtémoc accepted defeat:

> Ah, Captain, I have done everything in my power to defend my country and keep it out of your hands. And since my luck has not been good, I beg you to end my life. That would be just. And with that you can finish with the Mexican kingdom since you have destroyed and killed my city and my vassals.

Rather than kill him, however, Cortés preferred to keep the new Aztec emperor alive in captivity in order to quell any subsequent revolt. It was not until 1525 that the last Aztec emperor was accused of plotting a revolt and hanged.

So it was that by mid-1521, two years after their first arrival, Cortés and his army were in control of a city in ruins and a people who had seen their worst prophecies fulfilled. Estimates of the losses on the Spanish side vary between 500 and 1,000 out of a total of 1,800 men. On the Aztec side, as many as 100,000 are said to have died. The remaining indigenous population were the subjects of a new and distant emperor. Forced to worship a new deity, their ancient way of life had vanished forever.

3 Spanish Colonial Rule

Much of the city of Tenochtitlán was destroyed during the final resistance by the Aztecs under Cuauhtémoc. Hernán Cortés at first favoured creating a new city in a different location, but the wealth of building material available from the ruins and the fact that, as the Spaniards had learnt to their cost, the city on the lakes was easily defensible soon led him to change his mind.

Cortés then ordered the construction of the Spanish capital directly on top of the Aztec one, with the Templo Mayor at its centre. While Cortés retired south to his palace outside the city in Coyoacán, the rebuilding began at once. According to the Franciscan friar Motolinia in *Historia de las Indias de Nueva España*:

> the seventh plague was the rebuilding of the great city of Mexico, in which more people were involved than in the construction of the temple of Jerusalem . . . some people were crushed by beams, others fell from up above, others took material from demolished buildings in one spot to rebuild in another, especially when they tore down the main temples of the demons. Many indians [*sic*] died during this work.

The authority of this new capital was confirmed in October 1522 by a decree from Charles v, which gave the local *cabildo*, or administration, the right to construct all types of building, streets and roads. Mexico – or New Spain, as it was baptized – officially became a viceroyalty with wide powers of self-government. For the next three centuries, Mexico City was at the heart of a vast empire that

MEXICO.

MEXICO. REGIA
ET CELEBRIS
HISPANIAE NO-
VAE CIVITAS.

Early map of Mexico-Tenochtitlán, attributed to Cortés.

stretched from California in the north to Honduras in the south.
Much of the wealth produced throughout this vast empire, and most
of the colonial administration, was based in the Mexican capital.
(For almost five centuries, no ruler from Spain ever visited this new
land. It was not until 1991 that King Juan Carlos of Spain came to
visit Guadalajara in Mexico for the first Ibero-American meeting of
heads of state.)

Cortés handed the task of laying out the new capital to one
Alonso García Bravo. His design kept the outline of the old streets,
and followed the by now traditional gridiron pattern, divided into
blocks, or *manzanas*, with eighteen streets running north–south
crossed by seven from east to west, and seven squares, with the Plaza
Mayor (now the Zócalo) at its heart. The triumphant conquistadors
were of course given pride of place: Cortés himself had two huge
palaces built on the edge of the central square, mostly from the volcanic tezontle bricks of Moctezuma's own palaces. His fellow soldiers
were granted similar grandiose buildings nearby. There were strict
rules about the height of these residences and the kind of facades
that were permitted. Different areas were allotted to different functions, with zones for trade, administration, churches and schools.

The surviving indigenous population were permitted to build
further out from the city centre in *barrios* similar in size to the four
Aztec quadrants of Tenochtitlán, but now renamed after Christian
saints and with a church in a central square. The early Spanish city
is thought to have had some 30,000 inhabitants, with little more
than a thousand of Spanish origin. The Aztec canals were retained
as a means of communication, and a shipyard was built for the
construction of brigantines to ply the five surrounding lakes.

Cortés himself did not enjoy the glories of the rebuilt city for
long. In 1528 he was summoned back to Spain to face charges of abuse
of authority during his years in Mexico. He was replaced by imperial
officials, or an *audiencia*, which is seen by the writer Jonathan Kandell
in *La Capital: The Biography of Mexico City* as ushering in

the most despotic and corrupt period of colonial government in
New Spain. Guzmán [the head of the *audiencia*] ordered the

The first viceroy of New Spain, Antonio de Mendoza.

enslavement of large numbers of Indians and a heavy increase in the tributes and forced labor required from them. Spaniards who still supported Cortés were imprisoned or executed, and their properties and *encomiendas* were turned over to Guzmán's allies.

Despite this, writing in his book *New Spain*, Nicolas Cheetham, a twentieth-century British ambassador to Mexico, comes to a somewhat surprising conclusion. He argues that if any other European power had discovered the new territories of Mexico, the indigenous peoples would probably have suffered even more. 'After the horrors of conquest,' Cheetham writes, 'they would have had to endure the sufferings of colonial rule without the advantage of any of its redeeming or palliative features. At the worst they could have been systematically wiped out, like their cousins further to the north.' Instead, he argues, there was a fusion of cultures that eventually gave rise to the unique mixture that is Mexico.

In 1535 Charles v appointed the first viceroy, Antonio de Mendoza. The government of New Spain and its capital had passed once and for all from the generation of the adventurers of the conquest to one of loyal servants of the Spanish crown. Although Cortés was cleared of the charges against him and returned to Mexico in 1530, he had no chance of regaining power there. He returned to Spain a disappointed man, and died outside Seville in 1547.

Viceroy Mendoza was a Renaissance humanist who sought to improve Mexico City along classical lines. Under his rule the first printing press in the Americas was set up in 1535, and in 1551 the first university was founded. Schooling was undertaken by Dominican and Franciscan friars, notably at a centre in the northern suburb of Tlatelolco, where the surviving Aztec nobility were taught.

At the same time, Mendoza's view of the city rapidly constructed under Cortés was harsh. He wrote back to the emperor in Spain:

> As far as the construction of the monasteries and public buildings goes, there have been great errors, because neither in their plans nor in the rest has what was desirable been followed, because no one knew what should be done or how to do these things correctly. To rectify this, I agreed with the friars of Saint Francis and Saint Augustine on a rational plan for the city, and now all buildings follow it.

Under Mendoza's rule, the streets and squares were widened and straightened to form straight lines and emphasize the chequerboard pattern common to Spanish cities in the New World, soon to be codified under the new emperor Felipe II in the *Ordenanzas de poblaciones*. Many of the Aztec canals were filled in, and new churches and convents constructed in the classical Renaissance style, in which grace and harmony replaced the need for the fortifications and solidity of Cortés's time.

In 1562 the Spanish viceroy took over one of Cortés's palaces on the north side of the Plaza Mayor. This became the seat of government, the viceroy's residence, the royal mint and a garrison for troops. The square outside was used as a market for goods imported from Europe and also to stage religious festivals in front of the cathedral, the construction of which began in 1525.

By the end of the sixteenth century the city was so well established that the poet Bernardo de Balbuena wrote an epic poem, *Grandeza Mexicana* (The Greatness of Mexico), in its honour. The opening stanza outlines his view of the city's splendour:

> Of famed Mexico the seat,
> Origin and greatness of buildings
> Horses, streets, manners, fulfillment
> Words, virtues, variety of trades,

An imaginary view of the Mexican capital in the 17th century.

Gifts, happy occasions,
Immortal spring and its signs
Illustrious government, religion, state
All are numbered in this discourse.

Throughout the sixteenth and seventeenth centuries, the *peninsulares*, or nobles and officials born in Spain, continued to occupy the highest positions and reside in the most magnificent dwellings.

Spanish colonial society was built on a sharp pyramid, with the *peninsulares* at the top; a larger number of *creoles*, or Spaniards born in Mexico, on a lower level; then a larger number of *mestizos*, or mixed-race people; and at the bottom the indigenous peoples. They were kept from any high office or profession, largely denied access to the society ruled by the whiter-skinned inhabitants, and yet they were not allowed to develop according to their own traditions. A 1689 census shows that there were then approximately 5,000 *peninsulares* living in Mexico City, whose total population was somewhere in the region of 50,000, including the indigenous population, the growing number of *mestizos* and several thousand black slaves. Thomas Gage, a visitor from Britain in the early seventeenth century, includes these slaves in his portrait of the lively scene in the Alameda Central park:

> The gallants of the city shew themselves daily, some on horse-back and most in coaches, about four o'clock in the afternoon in a pleasant shady field called La Alameda, full of trees and walks . . . where do meet about two thousand coaches full of gallants, ladies, and citizens, to see and be seen, to court and be courted, the gentlemen having their train of blackamoor slaves, some a dozen, some half a dozen waiting on them, in brave and gallant liveries, heavy with gold and silver lace, with silk stockings on their black legs, and roses on their feet, and swords by their sides.

The *peninsulares'* wealth was often based on silver mines or the huge landholdings and haciendas that they owned, often hundreds of kilometres from Mexico City. The capital remained the centre through which nearly all trade and business passed, as well as being the heart of the thriving colony's political and social life. This established a pattern of dominance of the capital over the countryside and other cities that continues to this day. One of the more unfortunate effects of this is the resentment felt in the rest of Mexico towards the inhabitants of the capital, who are known as *chilangos* by those who see them as snobbish and divorced from the reality of the rest of Mexican society.

The Alameda park in the 18th century.

The rapid growth of the new capital brought fresh problems, which have persisted into the twenty-first century. As the forests surrounding the lakes were chopped down for construction and fuel, the lakes gradually silted up. This led to an increased danger of flooding, which culminated in the great flood of 1629. A large part of the city was under water for as long as five years, and all goods had to be carried by canoe. Those who could fled to neighbouring cities and towns, but several thousand of the native Indian population are thought to have died as a result of the inundation. A transfer of the viceroyalty to nearby Puebla was considered, but in the end the vested interests of the capital won out. It was after this natural

The 18th-century Casa de los Azulejos (House of Tiles), on the Callejón de la Condesa.

The House of Tiles

One of the most striking buildings from the centuries of Spanish rule is the Palace of the Counts of the Valle de Orizaba, better known as the 'House of Tiles'. Situated just west of the Zócalo on Calle Madero, it had one of the original canals running alongside it. Its name is due to its startling exterior, which is entirely covered in blue and white tiles.

After the Spanish conquest the building was one of the first palaces constructed in the new capital. In a painting of 1650 the counts' residence is clearly visible as a two-storey palace with crenellations that are more decorative than defensive. The present building dates from the eighteenth century, when it acquired its unique tiles. One legend has it that a desperate father complained to his dissipated son, 'You'll never make a house of tiles', whereupon the boy reformed and was so successful he covered the outside walls in tiles to prove his father wrong. Another more prosaic but possibly more truthful legend has it that one of the palace's female owners so admired the blue and white Talavera tile decorations typical of the nearby city of Puebla that she insisted on thousands being specially made for her own residence.

The house remained in the same family until the 1880s. A few years later, it was the seat of Mexico's Jockey Club, where members indulged in not only betting on horses but all kinds of gambling. This episode in the palace's history came to an abrupt end with the outbreak of the Mexican revolution in 1910; by 1915 it became no less than the 'House of the World's Workers', where the new emerging anarchist and socialist trade unions were headquartered.

In 1919 the House of Tiles underwent yet another transformation, into a guise that has lasted until today. This was thanks to the Sanborn brothers, who earlier in the century had come from the United States to sell ice cream in Mexico. They took over the empty building and turned it into a restaurant, coffee shop, pharmacy and bookshop. The interior patio was turned into the restaurant, but the eighteenth-century staircase up to the first floor survived, together with the coat of arms of the Orizaba family.

disaster – the first of many to afflict the city over the centuries – that the lakes were systematically drained and a canal, or *desagüe*, dug to take the sewage and other waters out of the enclosed Valley of Mexico and down towards the Pacific Ocean. Nevertheless, the threat of flooding during the rainy months from May to October persisted.

In 1900 the champion of progress and modernity Porfirio Díaz triumphantly inaugurated the Gran Canal, designed to resolve the problem once and for all. Unfortunately for him, this was followed a year later by further massive flooding, which continued until well past the middle of the twentieth century. The writer Elena Ponia-towska recalls a scene from her youth in the 1950s in *El último guajolote* (The Last Turkey):

> the central streets of 16 de Septiembre and Venustiano Carranza were flooded, and so a system of porters was set up for the young ladies who worked in the nearby Banco de Londres y México. But since the lady clerks did not want to be carried in somebody else's arms as though they were a loving couple, pressing against each other's chests, the porters had to tie a chair on their backs, and the princesses would climb on. For the modest sum of two pesos, they would find themselves delivered safe and sound on the other side.

Despite these problems, by the eighteenth century Mexico City was by far the largest and richest city in North America. The fortress-style early buildings had mostly been replaced by more luxurious mansions, which were both residences for the wealthy and powerful, and places where the family business was carried out. Often they were rectangular two-storey constructions built around one or two interior patios. The ground floor contained shops rented out or run by the family to sell produce from their haciendas or imported goods. The main entrance was designed so that horses and carriages could enter the central patio. From here, an often elab-orate stone staircase led up to the arcaded first floor, which was where the family lived, ate and had their offices. The main salon looked out over the street, the family bedrooms occupied the two wings and at the rear was the dining room, closer to the kitchens (which were housed in the back patios where the servants were lodged). The flat roofs often had small gardens and provided views over the city. Several of these palaces have survived into the twenty-first century. Perhaps the finest example is the Palacio de Iturbide on Calle Madero, with its magnificent stone doorway. Nowadays it is the Palacio de Cultura Banamex, where modern art exhibitions are frequently staged.

Beyond the city of palaces, the Indians and *mestizos* still lived in houses very similar to those they had occupied during the Aztec empire: single-storey huts made of adobe, with flat roofs and tiny windows. The system of *chinampas*, or floating islands, still functioned, and provided the capital's inhabitants with produce and flowers. Most of these common people lived in miserable conditions. In the second half of the eighteenth century a visiting priest from Spain was shocked at the poverty he saw: 'If we counted all the wretched of Spain, we would not find among them as many

The colonial palace where Emperor Iturbide resided.

Detail of the stonework on the Palacio de Iturbide.

naked people as there are in Mexico City,' he remarked. 'Of every one hundred people you come across, only one is properly clothed and wears shoes.'

At the dawn of the nineteenth century Mexico City boasted some 135,000 inhabitants. During an 1803 visit by the German naturalist and polymath Alexander von Humboldt, he was as impressed as the earlier conquistadors had been with the view of the city from afar:

> The city appears as if washed by the waters of Lake Texcoco, whose basin, surrounded with villages and hamlets, brings to mind the most beautiful lakes of the mountains of Switzerland. Large avenues of elms and poplars lead in every direction to the capital; and the two aqueducts, constructed over arches of very great elevation, cross the plain.

However, the inequalities of the colonial society were soon to lead to revolt both in the capital and in the countryside. In spite of the vast riches sent from Mexico, the rest of Latin America and its other overseas colonies, Spain itself was in crisis. From the 1760s onwards, strenuous attempts were made to modernize the administration of its colonies, foremost among them Mexico. This saw a reinforcement of Spanish influence in the Mexican capital, and led to the construction of such notable buildings as the Academy of San Carlos and the Palace of Mining in the centre of the city. The viceroy Count Revillagigedo set about renewing the central square, paving over the open sewers, getting rid of the sprawling market

Aztec statue of the goddess Coatlicue at the National Museum of Anthropology.

and introducing lighting. It was during these works that the most spectacular archaeological discoveries were made: the massive Piedra de Sol (Sunstone) showing the Aztec calendar, and the beautiful stone figure of the moon goddess Coatlicue (both of them now in the National Museum of Anthropology).

In spite of these efforts at renewal abroad, the Habsburg dynasty was crumbling and losing power in Europe. When Napoleon's forces entered Madrid and deposed the Spanish emperor in 1807, this was the signal for independence movements throughout Latin America to push for freedom. In Mexico, amid cries of ¡*Fuera los gachupines!* (Out with the Spaniards!), patriots took up the banner of revolt against colonial rule that after more than a decade of struggle was to lead to the creation of an independent Mexico.

4 Independence and Reaction

In 1799 there were riots in Mexico City against rule by the Spanish Bourbons, but over the next decade the struggle for independence from Spain spread mostly through the countryside under leaders such as Father Miguel Hidalgo. It was he who led the fight against the Spaniards in 1810, and his famous 'Cry of Dolores' – 'Viva Mexico! Long Live our Lady of Guadalupe! Death to bad government! Death to the *gachupines*!' – is still proclaimed on the evening of 15 September, before Independence Day celebrations the following day. In Mexico City, huge crowds gather in the Zócalo to watch the incumbent president emerge onto the balcony of the National Palace, ring a bell and repeat three times 'Viva Mexico!' as he waves the national flag. This ceremony is repeated in the 31 states of Mexico alongside Mexico City, and in Mexican embassies and consulates all over the world.

Back in 1810, however, this was merely the beginning of the battle for independence. The capital, with its many Spanish-born nobles and officials, remained loyal to the viceroy. Eventually, though, the forces supporting the Spanish crown were defeated, and in 1821 Mexico's independence from Spain was proclaimed in the southern town of Iguala. Even then the capital was still ruled – nominally at least – by the Spanish viceroy, the wonderfully named Juan O'Donojú. Over the next few months his position proved impossible, and he relinquished his authority to the Mexican general Agustín de Iturbide. A *cabildo* was set up to thrash out a constitution for the fledgling state, but attempts to establish a Mexican republic similar to that of the United States foundered when Iturbide was enthroned as emperor by popular acclaim.

Iturbide's empire was to last less than a year. In March 1823 he was deposed by other members of the army, led by a young *criollo* called Antonio López de Santa Anna. Iturbide was pensioned off and went to live in exile, first in Italy and then in England. On hearing rumours in the early months of 1824 that the Spaniards were about to attempt to regain control of the former colony, Iturbide set off for Mexico with his wife and children. He was arrested and shot by firing squad five days later. It was not until the following decade, in 1839, that his valuable role in the fight for independence was recognized, and his ashes were transferred to the cathedral in Mexico City.

After his fall from power, a new constitution was adopted, and Mexico was declared a republic. By 1825 the remaining Spaniards were forced to leave, but for several decades both the capital and the country as a whole lived through periods of great instability and conflict. Over the next three decades the nascent republic saw some fifty governments, which struggled to exert control over very different regions that were often run by local caudillos suspicious of the central power of Mexico City, its politicians, bureaucrats, rich

Mexican infantry marching by the National Palace and the Cathedral at Independence Day festivities, 16 September 1919.

merchants and businessmen. A vivid picture of the life and customs of Mexico City at this time is provided by Fanny Calderón de la Barca (born Frances Erskine Inglis in Edinburgh in 1804), the wife of the first ambassador sent by Spain to the newly recognized republic. She describes how her rich and powerful friends avoided the dirt and turmoil of the capital's streets in her *Life in Mexico*:

> A few ladies in black gowns and mantillas do occasionally venture forth on foot very early to shop or to attend mass [but] the streets are so ill-kept, the pavements so narrow, the crowd so great, and the multitude of beggars in rags and blankets so annoying, that all these inconveniences, added to the heat of the sun in the middle of the day, form a perfect excuse for their non-appearance in the streets of Mexico.

General Antonio López de Santa Anna was a central figure throughout these years. Born in the Xalapa in 1794, he was at first an officer in the Spanish army but during the struggle for independence he changed sides and fought for those Mexicans seeking liberation. He was seen as such a hero that in 1833, following the overthrow of the empire under Agustín de Iturbide, he was elected as president of the new republic of Mexico. It was not long before he proclaimed himself dictator, bypassing the reform-minded Congress. In 1836 he took command of the army against the Texans who wanted to free their state from Mexican rule, and defeated them at the famous Battle of the Alamo. His victory was short-lived, as his army was routed a few months later by a larger U.S. force, and this defeat also led to him losing power back in Mexico. But by 1838 he was back in charge and was soon fighting again, this time against the French, in what became known as the 'Pastry War', when the French sent troops to the port of Veracruz to back up their demands for reparations following the looting of a French baker's shop in Mexico City and other attacks on French citizens. During the battle for Veracruz, Santa Anna was wounded in the left leg and had to have most of it amputated.

Despite the Mexican army's eventual surrender to the French forces, General Santa Anna was seen as a national hero. He returned

General Scott leading American troops into Mexico City, 14 September 1847.

to the capital, and it was not long before he was appointed president again. He ordered the remains of his leg to be dug up from its burial place on his hacienda and reburied with full military honours in the Santa Paula Pantheon in Mexico City.

When a few years later the United States annexed Texas, Santa Anna again declared war, with even more disastrous results. By September 1847 U.S. troops had occupied the Mexican capital, and Mexico was forced to agree to the sale to the United States of not only Texas but California, Utah, Nevada, Arizona and New Mexico to ensure their withdrawal. At a stroke, Mexico lost half the territory it had controlled under Spanish rule, and resentment towards the 'giant of the north' was created, the effects of which are still plain today.

When Mexico again went to war with the United States in 1848, Santa Anna and his men were surprised at lunch one day by a detachment of U.S. soldiers from Illinois. Although Santa Anna managed to escape, his false leg (he had replaced his lost leg with a prosthetic made of cork) was taken away – today it is on display in the Illinois State Military Museum in Springfield.

Nor was that the end of the story for Santa Anna's buried leg. In the 1840s and '50s Santa Anna was in and out of power almost continuously (in total he was head of the Mexican government no fewer than eleven times). Back in the presidency in 1853, he by now titled himself the 'Most Serene Highness' and had brought in many repressive, reactionary measures. When he was finally overthrown by the liberals under the great reformer Benito Juárez, crowds broke into the Santa Paula Pantheon and exhumed his leg, 'playing with it and taking their rage out on it', as one Mexican historian has written. After further years in exile, Santa Anna was allowed to return to Mexico in 1874. By then he was a spent force and in ill health. He died a poor man in Mexico City at the age of 82.

Some thirty years after independence, Mexico City was poorer and less influential than it had been under the Spaniards. The population was by now an estimated 200,000, swollen by the thousands of poor peasants fleeing the violence and the desperate working conditions on the big haciendas in the countryside. Only a small proportion of these newcomers could find work, and this was the start of the infamous slums, or *vecindades*, that came to ring the centre of the city, in places such as Tepito or the Candelaria de los Patos. Journalists such as Ignacio Altamirano in the 1860s described the misery in La Candelaria, pushing for reforms:

The storming of Chapultepec, 13 September 1847.

Slums in Tepito.

Nearly all the houses are tenements containing hundreds of tiny rooms, let by the month at a rent that varies between four *reales* and two *pesos*. Many of them are no bigger than six square feet; it seems impossible that a family of six or eight persons could live there. They are little more than coffins where the poor bury their anguish as they wait for death. Old people, women and children sleep on ancient blackened floors; mud from the lake constantly oozes through the cracks. We visited many such dungeons where society's disinherited serve out the sentence of destiny.

The Mexican economy was still based on the export of minerals and agricultural produce, but with the loss of guaranteed trade with Spain, both the capital and the country were in the doldrums. It was not until Santa Anna was finally ousted that attempts were made by such liberal reformers as Benito Juárez from Oaxaca to modernize the state. A new constitution was brought in, and in 1856 the Ley Lerdo, or Lerdo Law, stripped the Catholic Church of some of its privileges. Churches and other church-owned properties not in regular use were seized. This led to the demolition of many of the most ancient churches in Mexico City, such as San Francisco, while convents were converted into housing or warehouses. In *The City of Palaces: Chronicle of Lost Heritage*, the historian of Mexico City Guillermo Tovar de Teresa describes the destruction caused:

> In 1861, a true 'feat' was performed: dozens of buildings were demolished in just a few months. The inhabitants of the city grew accustomed to the sound of pickaxes and crowbars, the crash of collapsing buildings, and other typical sounds of demo-lition. Soldiers entered San Agustín with ropes and pulled down the burnished gold and polychromed figures of the main altarpiece, which smashed as they hit the ground. They destroyed the altarpieces with axes and at time used horses to ply them from the walls.

A tenement in the early 20th century.

View of the city towards the east, *c.* 1855.

The loss of links with Spain had been replaced by capital and investment from the more industrialized European nations of Great Britain, France and Germany. As president in 1861, Juárez decreed that Mexico could no longer pay its debts to France or Great Britain, the industrialized European countries that had replaced Spain as the providers of capital and investment following the ousting of the Spaniards. Almost immediately the countries sent troops to 'persuade' the Mexican authorities to change their mind. The British forces soon withdrew, but the French defeated Juárez's forces and marched on Mexico City, where according to the French general Forey: 'the entire population of this capital welcomed us with an enthusiasm verging on delirium. The soldiers of France were literally crushed under the garlands and nosegays.'

At the time, France was ruled by the emperor Napoleon III. He was keen to regain French influence in the Americas to counterbalance the growing power of the United States, and so came up with the disastrous idea of sending the Habsburg Archduke Maximilian I to become emperor of the Mexicans, protected by the French army. Maximilian and his wife Carlota (daughter of the Belgian king) disembarked in Veracruz on 28 May 1864. The new European emperor celebrated the occasion grandiloquently, remarking: 'Mexicans, you have called for me; a spontaneous majority among you has chosen me to watch over your destinies from this day forward. I submit myself joyfully to that call.'

Maximilian and his young bride were received joyously in the Mexican capital. They established their home high on Chapultepec Hill, where Maximilian soon ordered the construction of a replica of his beloved Miramare Castle back in Trieste. In the park he had a lake dug, thousands of trees planted and roads built around the hill. 'It's the Schönbrunn of Mexico,' he wrote. 'An enchanting palace built on a basalt outcrop surrounded by the famous, beautiful trees planted by Moctezuma, and the view is so beautiful it can only be compared to that of Sorrento.' For their journeys into the centre of the old city, the couple also oversaw the construction of a wide avenue (now the Paseo de la Reforma) which Carlota based on the magnificent Avenue Louise of her native Brussels.

The imperial couple brought in a taste for all things European, but the love affair with the Mexican people, if it had ever really existed, was quickly over. Faced with mounting hostility from Mexican forces, Napoleon III withdrew the French troops, and Maximilian and the conservatives who backed him were left to face Juárez and a growing number of Mexicans who wanted to rule their own destinies. In 1867 Maximilian was captured during the defence of Querétaro. Despite international pleas for mercy, Juárez had him shot by firing squad at dawn on 19 June. Carlota, who had already left Mexico City to return to Europe, became increasingly mentally unstable and lived for a further sixty years as a recluse in a Belgian chateau.

Now it was Juárez's turn to enter the Mexican capital in triumph. Mexico was once again a republic, and he was its president. The capital he ruled over was said by a contemporary chronicler to consist of more than 4,000 solid stone houses of one or two storeys, in addition to many thousands more humble adobe dwellings, some

The monument to the 'Boy Heroes' in Chapultepec.

THE NIÑOS HÉROES AND THEIR MONUMENT

During the U.S. incursion under General Winfield Scott into the Mexican capital in September 1847, their troops met stubborn resistance on Chapultepec Hill. This was where the Mexican military academy was situated, and the site from which a few officers and a small band of cadets aged between thirteen and nineteen bravely defended their positions for several hours. When the order to retreat was given, six of them refused to withdraw and reportedly leapt to their deaths instead. Legend has it that one of them, Juan Escutia, was so patriotic that he wrapped himself in the Mexican standard that had been fluttering over the academy and threw himself off the top of the escarpment rather than allowing the flag to fall into the hands of the marauding U.S. troops.

After the battle, the remains of the cadets and others who had died in the fighting were buried in common graves at the foot of Chapultepec Hill. In 1881 a monument was built nearby in honour of the six fallen cadets. A century after the conflict, in 1947, the remains of the six cadets were discovered in one of these graves, although as so often with regard to history in Mexico, doubts were immediately raised over whether these in fact belonged to the six boys. Nevertheless, the remains were placed in separate urns and a plaque was dedicated to their memory. In 1952 a large marble monument dedicated to those who had died in the 1846–7 war was inaugurated as the Altar a la Patria (Altar of the Fatherland). The semicircular memorial was topped with six urns said to contain the ashes of the six *Niños Héroes*, or Boy Heroes, and nowadays the monument, at the end of the Paseo de la Reforma and one of the main entrances to Chapultepec Park, is commonly seen as a shrine to them and their courage. The six child heroes have figured on coins and banknotes, and have many streets in the capital and other cities named after them. Each year 13 September is a national holiday in their honour.

A *pulquería* in Mexico City, 1881, wood engraving.

five hundred stores, 84 cafes and many more cantinas and *pulquerías* selling cheap pulque alcohol distilled from the agave plant.

Juárez began to push through political reforms and to modernize and clean up the capital. Links with the rest of the country were improved and Mexico City entered the railway age with the inauguration of the railway from the Gulf Coast port of Veracruz to the heart of the capital. When Juárez was re-elected president in 1871, it seemed that Mexico could at last look forward to a period of democracy and economic progress, but his death a year later brought another twist to the fortunes of capital and country.

The Fine Arts Palace.

5 The Porfiriato

B enito Juárez's untimely death in 1872, only a year after he had been re-elected president, led to yet another period of uncertainty for Mexico. Eventually one of his army colleagues in the fight against the French, José de la Cruz Porfirio Díaz Mori, came to the fore. Although he had earlier been on the side of those calling for political reform and had stood in 1872 on a platform of 'no re-election', once he had used his military strength to overthrow the elected president Lerdo de Tejada in 1876, Díaz had himself re-elected no fewer than seven times. Stepping down in 1880 only to allow one of his placemen to keep the presidential throne warm for him, he held on to power for more than three decades until unseated by the violent revolution that began in 1910.

His rule remains one of the most controversial periods in recent Mexican history. With his slogan of 'Order, Peace and Progress' he brought stability to a country that had seen as many as fifty governments in the decades since independence. He suppressed regional uprisings and banditry in the countryside, using his *rurales* police to dispense often very rough justice, but succeeded in unifying the nation. The all-important mining industry was overhauled thanks to the injection of foreign capital, and ports were built or modernized to help export the minerals. Land ownership was contracted in many fewer hands, bringing more up-to-date methods of agriculture and livestock rearing, and the production of export crops such as tobacco, sugar and coffee. As a result, however, as many as 200,000 peasants were forced off their lands. The vast majority of them flooded into Mexico City and other large urban centres.

In the period between 1870 and 1910 the capital grew to almost five times the size it had been at the start of the century, and at the turn of the twentieth century had more than half a million inhabitants out of a national total of some 15 million. Foreign trade increased more than tenfold during the Porfiriato, with much of the wealth staying in the capital. The big landowners also preferred to reside most of the year in the fashionable districts of Mexico City, and to spend their money there.

With the slogan of 'Poca política, mucha administración' (little politics, a lot of administration), Díaz brought in a team of *científicos* (who might nowadays be known as 'technocrats') to pursue

Women in El Buen Tono cigarette factory.

The young general
Porfirio Díaz in the
1870s.

progressive policies for the economy, industry and other areas of
national life. These *científicos* adopted the fashionable French
'positivist' philosophy that rejected abstract notions in favour of
'scientifically' planned solutions in all areas of public life. This was
an era of a proliferation of committees, commissions and government agencies that often produced wide-ranging plans for reform
in all areas, most of which were never acted on. Porfirio Díaz ruled
as an autocrat, usually designating the candidates who sat in Congress,
and himself being the only candidate when the presidency was
renewed every four years. He undermined the judiciary, and curbed
the independence of the press and intellectuals. He allowed the Catholic Church to regain influence, and kept the army quiet by means
of bribes and land concessions.

Chicken sellers in the city, *c*. 1910.

Family of labourers, newly arrived in the city, c. 1906.

Mexico City's place at the centre of this rapidly changing country became even more essential. Some 80 per cent of government spending on infrastructure and utilities went to improving the capital. According to Michael Johns in *The City of Mexico in the Age of Díaz*, 'The country's few large importers worked out of modified colonial palaces and new office buildings to supply the capital with European and American goods . . . fully one third of Mexico's small class of manufacturers (textiles, shoes, cigarettes etc) operated in the capital.' At the same time, the number of people working for the state increased spectacularly, the vast majority of them concentrated in the capital. This created a practice and a culture of people being dependent on the state for their livelihoods that has continued and even been reinforced well into the twenty-first century.

The Buenavista railway station (opened in 1873), linking Mexico City with the port of Veracruz.

The last three decades of the nineteenth century were the age of communications. The most powerful symbol of this were the railways, which grew from only a few hundred kilometres at the start of the 1870s to some 19,000 kilometres (12,000 mi.) spanning the entire country by the dawn of the twentieth century. The capital was the hub of the system. Five new railway stations bore witness to its spectacular growth and became noted landmarks in the centre of the city. Although the station for Ferrocarriles Mexicanos was finished in 1873, before Porfirio was elected president (the railway reduced the time taken to reach the port of Veracruz on the Gulf Coast from several days to thirteen hours) another four terminals were built following English or French styles. They soon became striking landmarks, especially the Buenavista Station that served Ciudad Juárez in the far north of the country.

However, possibly the most outstanding examples of this new age of speed and progress were the Palacio de Correos, a neo-Venetian palace begun in 1902, and the Palacio de Comunicaciones y Obras Públicas, both of them built in the historic centre of the city

Inside the Palacio de Correos.

and replacing much older buildings: Porfirio was determined to look forwards rather than backwards. At the same time, the new fashion for department stores saw the construction of iron and glass palaces of commerce such as the Palacio de Hierro or the capital's most elegant jewellery store, La Esmeralda.

Street lighting, gas and electricity were brought in. By 1892 the central Alameda Park was remodelled, cleared of beggars and the homeless, and brightly lit with new electric lighting. Avenues and roads were widened in an attempt to emulate Paris. Trams, first horse-drawn and later electric, sped along the new highways. One of the main innovations was the widening of the Paseo de la Reforma leading to Chapultepec, with new roundabouts built in honour of Columbus and Cuauhtémoc (but significantly, in what nowadays would be seen as an example of political correctness, not the conquistador Hernán Cortés). The centre point of this elegant avenue was the Angel de la Independencia. This is a tall column topped with

Statue of Diana the Huntress.

a golden angel holding a victory wreath in one hand and the broken chains of tyranny in the other. Typically, the bronze statue was created by a Mexican designer who had studied in Paris, and the statue was cast there. As with so many of the capital's more grandiose monuments, construction of the 36-metre-high (118-ft) column, topped by its golden angel, ran into great difficulties due to the soft soil of the dried-out lake bed underneath.

In the twentieth century, two further monuments have been erected beyond the Angel. These are a statue of Diana the Huntress – which caused a scandal when it was inaugurated in 1942 because the Greek goddess was naked – and a large fountain dedicated to Petróleos Mexicanos in commemoration of the nationalization of the country's oil resources in 1938, which was added in 1952. Perhaps the most regrettable addition was made in 2012, when the so-called Estela de Luz (Pillar of Light) was finally inaugurated at the entrance to Chapultepec Park, almost a year and a half late as it was intended to commemorate the bicentenary of the fight for independence. The avenue is also flanked with more than seventy statues of prominent figures of the 1860s Reform movement.

The development of the Paseo de la Reforma during the Porfiriato was a sign of how the capital was growing and breaking the bounds of the old colonial city. Following the Ley Lerdo that limited the power and properties of the Catholic Church, many wealthy families chose to move out of the old historic centre and reside in buildings previously owned by the Church in the north and west, close to Reforma and Chapultepec. New neighbourhoods sprung up for the middle classes too, as in Colonia San Rafael and Santa María. The residents here could enjoy running water and sewage and drainage systems previously only rarely found in the colonial city. The physical distance between classes in the capital became more pronounced. Whereas in the colonial city the different strata of the capital's society shared the central area more or less harmoniously, now the urban space became divided between west and east in a way that is still marked today. As Manuel Torres Torija wrote in 1906:

The Fine Arts Palace auditorium and Tiffany stage curtain.

The Fine Arts Palace

This palace dedicated to the arts of drama, opera and painting was originally intended as a symbol of the modern, progressive rule of the strongman Porfirio Díaz. However, by the time of its completion it had come much more to represent the solidity (and possibly the confused sense of taste) of the regime that emerged out of the years of violent revolution in the late 1920s. It took from 1932 to September 1934 to complete, and although the impression it gives is of massive solidity, like many of the large buildings in the centre of the city it has sunk into the soft subsoil so that instead of going up to the entrance the visitor has to descend to its level. The white Carrara marble facade is decorated with heavy sculptures, with a specially designed crystal roof in the centre.

The palace's interior is an extraordinary Art Deco creation, from the pre-Hispanic panels and arches to the elaborate wrought iron-work on the balconies, ticket office and staircases. In addition to the exhibition halls, the first floor boasts murals by Rufino Tamayo (*Birth of our Nation*), while another floor up the walls are surrounded by vast murals by José Clemente Orozco, Siqueiros, Diego Rivera (a replica of his *Universal Man and the Machine*, originally intended for the Rockefeller Center in New York but which proved too revolutionary for its patrons there) and other Mexican artists of the day.

This decor is plainly intended to impress the visitor with the grandeur of the Mexican society that is being forged after the revolution. This impression continues inside the theatre itself, where the extravagance of the auditorium is matched by the proscenium stage, where masks of Tlaloc and Chaac, the Aztec water gods, are flanked by more mythical sculptures, and by the 22-ton Tiffany 'curtain', or sliding panel, which features a dazzling representation of Mexico City's tutelary volcanoes Popocatépetl and Iztaccihuatl in coloured glass. As the Mexican writer José Joaquín Blanco wrote of it in the 1980s: 'a crazy building, one so extraordinary that it goes beyond the wildest dreams of any utopian ideal of kitsch. It is more absurd, more ridiculous, more majestically antiquated, more pompous and more useless than any of our colonial churches, our folkloric dances, costumbrista novelists or regional dishes.'

There is a very marked difference between east and west Mexico [City]. The former is old, somber, narrow, often winding and always dirty, with miserable alleys, deserted and antiquated squares, ruined bridges, deposits of slimy water, and paltry adobe houses inhabited by squalid persons. The west is modern and cheerful, with open streets drawn at right angles that are clean, carefully paved and full of shady parks, gardens and squares; there is good drainage and the elegant houses, though at times in the worst architectural styles, are costly, imposing, and modern.

The eastern flank of the city, based around the parishes of the old colonial churches, was still largely a collection of one-storey adobe houses. They had small, glassless windows and small doors, leading directly on to beaten earth streets. One writer characterized what they contained inside: '[they] were furnished with a pine bed, a table, and a rickety chair or two. A picture calendar was stuck to a wall, a large earthenware water jar sat by the door, and one or two pegs in the wall held the family wardrobe.' The inhabitants here were usually peasants forced off their lands who came to the capital in search of whatever work they could find, usually as labourers, porters or workers in the small factories that were then springing up in the capital. The men still wore their countryside attire – cotton pants, *guaraches*, or plaited leather sandals, white cotton shirts and the stereotypical wide-brimmed sombreros – while the women wore their traditional long skirts, petticoats and colourful blouses. A visitor from the United States described these eastern parts of the city as 'an unhealthy world of filth, dirt and vice', and much of the violence and disorder has been attributed to the excessive consumption of pulque. This white, bitter alcoholic drink made from the maguey plant had always been a staple of life in the Mexican countryside, and now it increasingly spread to the poorer areas of the capital: according to Michael Johns, in 1864 there were 51 *pulquerías* where the alcoholic beverage was served, but more than 1,200 of them, practically one on every street corner in the poorer parts of the city, by 1905. According to T. Philip Terry, an English writer who visited the capital at the dawn of the century, these bars and the surrounding areas were 'thronged with blear-eyed, sodden male and female degenerates', while Johns states that as many as 85 per cent of those held overnight in police cells were there for being 'drunk and disorderly'.

These habits, a lack of proper work, crowded living conditions and a dearth of education, in what even the municipal administration called 'the most unhealthy city in the world', led to high levels of violence and meant that the death rate was twice that of other Latin American capitals such as Buenos Aires or Rio de Janeiro.

Porfirio Díaz could not or would not see the grim reality in which hundreds of thousands lived in both the capital and the Mexican countryside. For the 1910 centenary of the beginning of the fight for independence from Spain, he was concerned to show the world that Mexico was not only the equal of the other great cities of Latin America, but it could rival the United States and much of Europe. The crowning symbol of this sense of national pride was the Angel of Independence, inaugurated on 16 September 1910. But the most spectacular monument to Porfirio Díaz's three decades in power was not completed until long after his death in lonely exile in Paris in 1915. This was the outrageously pompous Palacio de Bellas Artes just to the west of the old historic centre, next to the Alameda Park. It was planned on a spot where for two centuries the Convent of Santa Isabel had stood, until it was deconsecrated in the late 1860s. In the 1880s the convent buildings were replaced by the Teatro Nacional, where the high society of the time went to watch dramas and operas. But the theatre was not spectacular enough for Porfirio Díaz, who wanted a venue for art that would outshine the Paris Opera. So in 1904 he laid the foundation stone for the new Palacio de Bellas Artes, to be designed by the Italian architect already responsible for the nearby Palacio de Correos. As with the Angel of Independence, however, the soft subsoil from the dried-out lakebed underneath would not support the intended huge cast-iron structure, and construction had not advanced very far when it was interrupted for almost twenty years. This was because although Porfirio Díaz's grip on power had seemed unshakeable for three decades, it too was built on unstable ground. The poverty and oppression in rural Mexico, the lack of political freedoms and the arbitrary nature of the regime's system of justice, and the increasingly glaring gulf between the rich and the poor so shocked John Kenneth Turner, the North American author of *Barbarous Mexico*, that he predicted in 1910 'that the tide of opposition, damned and held back as it has been by the army and secret police, is rising to a height where it must shortly overflow that dam'. His prediction swiftly came to pass. Within a few months, Porfirio Díaz and his repressive dictatorship had been swept away, leading to the decade of civil struggle known as the Mexican Revolution.

6 The Years of Revolution

In Mexico, political change can often be as violent as the eruptions of the volcanoes Popocatépetl and Iztaccíhuatl looming in the distance. In September 1910, Porfirio Díaz triumphantly celebrated the centenary of the battle for independence from Spain. Díaz seemed to think his regime could continue forever, and yet within a year he had been overthrown and dispatched into miserable exile in France, where he died soon afterwards. The struggle that convulsed Mexico this time was for free elections, greater social justice and, for the peasants in the countryside, the possibility to regain their plots of land that had been seized by the huge landowners. Achieving these aims was no easy task. It was more than a decade before the institutions and power structures of the Porfiriato had been swept away and a more democratic government under a unifying president put in their place. As many as a million Mexicans died in the struggle, which raged through the Mexican countryside and the capital year after year until 1920 and beyond.

In was in February 1911 that a small band of revolutionaries under Francisco I. Madero, who had been robbed of victory by the aged despot in the 1910 presidential election, crossed into Mexico from the United States with a small band of followers. He was soon joined by peasant armies led by charismatic leaders such as Emiliano Zapata in the south, with his slogan of 'Land and Freedom', and by Francisco 'Pancho' Villa in the north. At first, the violent combats with forces loyal to Díaz did not affect Mexico City directly, although each of the insurgent leaders swept into the capital to assert his authority. Often, however, these attempts did not last more than a few months.

Revolutionary leaders at the Hotel Coliseo, Mexico City, 24 June 1911. Emiliano Zapata is seated at centre.

Madero was the first to take over the presidential throne following Porfirio Díaz's ignominious flight. Cheered by huge crowds when he entered the capital in June 1911 (the same day that a powerful earthquake shook the city, which was seen as a good omen), he called general elections and was a clear winner of the presidential contest in November 1911. From the start, however, Madero came under attack from all sides: the conservative forces in both the capital and the countryside saw him as offering too many concessions to the rebels, while the revolutionaries under Villa and Zapata judged him to have gone back on his promises of radical reform. As the Mexican historian Enrique Krauze has written in his book *Redeemers*: 'In November 1911 Madero finally became president thanks to the freest, most spontaneous vote which he won with the biggest majority in recent Mexican history. He ruled for fifteen months, with so many problems that with hindsight his period in office seems like a miracle of survival.'

In February 1913 it was the conservative forces under General Victoriano Huerta who rose against him. This was when Mexico City felt the full force of the violent struggle, in what became known as the *Decena trágica* – the 'Tragic Ten Days' that saw more than a thousand people killed as the rival forces battled for supremacy on the streets of the capital. Madero had appointed General Huerta to lead the government forces when the previous army commander was killed by the insurgents in the National Palace, but Huerta was soon conspiring with Félix Díaz, the former dictator's nephew, and others to overthrow President Madero. The rebels took over the city's main arsenal at La Ciudadela in the centre of the city, while loyal troops shelled them from the National Palace and the Zócalo. On 18 February 1913, Madero and his vice president Pino Suárez were captured in a skirmish inside the National Palace and forced to resign. Huerta immediately declared himself president. Four days later, on the night of 22 February 1913, Madero and his deputy were bundled out of the National Palace, allegedly for transfer to Porfirio Díaz's new model Lecumberri Prison in the northern suburb of

Centre of the city during the 'Tragic Ten Days' of revolutionary turmoil in 1913.

Ministry of Education Murals

As the violence of the revolution subsided, intellectuals, writers and artists in the Mexican capital began to reinterpret the nation's past. They emphasized the uniqueness of Mexican culture, which had produced great civilizations over several thousand years, and was enriched by these indigenous traditions as well as those inherited from three hundred years of Spanish rule.

As part of this process, the minister of education in the early 1920s, José Vasconcelos, commissioned artists to depict scenes from this long history on the walls of public buildings. He wanted above all for ordinary Mexicans to be able to identify with their nation's struggles and glories.

Some of the most spectacular murals were painted in the new Ministry of Education building, completed in 1922 in the historic centre. Vasconcelos saw the architecture of the new ministry as representing the nobility of the task of educating the nation, saying: 'It should be a work in stone that is a moral organization, vast and complex, with big rooms in which one may hold free discussions under high ceilings where ideas may expand without any sense of obstruction.'

Several painters were invited to fill the walls with uplifting illustrations of several thousand years of Mexican history, but Diego Rivera soon made the project his own. Over three floors, he painted the 'Labour and Fiestas' of the Mexican people. The top floor presents no fewer than 21 frescos depicting workers and peasants celebrating the gains of the recent revolution, while the beastly bourgeois choke on their gold and covetousness. The staircases also lead the visitor from Mexico's tropical coastline, up through the high deserts, to the volcanic peaks. Above them all, Rivera painted himself as the great architect of this cosmic vision of Mexico's triumphs and tribulations.

Rivera's mural showing the Feast of the Day of the Dead.

Tlatelolco. A simulated attempt at escape by the two men was staged. This gave their escort the excuse to shoot both men out of hand up against the penitentiary wall.

General Huerta's rule was even briefer than Madero's. Venustiano Carranza, the commander of the Constitutional army in the north, rose against him, while in the south Zapata's guerrilla forces continued to fight against the central government. By July 1914 Huerta had been forced out of power, replaced by Carranza and his leading general, Álvaro Obregón. But Carranza's hold on power was even more tenuous, and when Pancho Villa's forces closed in on Mexico City from the north and those of Zapata from Morelos in the south, Carranza and his federal army withdrew from the capital. The city was occupied for weeks by the guerrilla fighters, although Zapata himself is said to have stayed only one night, complaining that the capital was so filthy it was uninhabitable.

By the time the rebel forces withdrew in early 1915, Mexico City was in a desperate state. Shortages of food and clean water led to several deadly epidemics; adult males constantly ran the risk of being press-ganged into one or other armed band; many hundreds of

Queuing for food during the revolution.

citizens suspected of supporting either Porfirio Díaz or Huerta were killed; churches were left empty and often ransacked. As the American author Jonathan Kandell has written:

> Sometimes scourged by famine and scarred by battle, and always swelled by refugees, Mexico City lived with a siege mentality. Many of its inhabitants viewed the Revolution as a maelstrom of peasant rabble sweeping out of the hinterlands and threatening to devastate their city.

Eventually General Obregón defeated Villa's forces in the north of the country, and Zapata's fighters to the south were gradually subdued. Over the following two years Obregón and Carranza consolidated their position; life in the capital gradually returned to a semblance of normality. A Constitutional Assembly was convened in December 1916, and a few months later a new national constitution was promulgated. This followed on from the 1857 Reform restricting the rights of the Catholic Church and limiting foreign investment. Education was to be free and secular. The 1917 constitution also brought in new labour rights and a land reform designed to restore ownership to peasants and small farmers who had been robbed of their landholdings under the Porfiriato. As the writer Manuel Gómez Morín put it a few years later: 'With optimistic consternation we became aware of unsuspected truths. Mexico existed. Mexico, a nation with possibilities, aspirations, with life and problems of its own.'

In March 1917 Venustiano Carranza was elected as the first president of the new republic. In Mexico City he worked to restore order and essential services such as clean water and electricity. Factories, shops and markets reopened, and police replaced the ragged revolutionaries on street corners. Carranza also sent forces to deal with the continuing threat from Zapata to the south of the capital, finally luring him to his death in an ambush in 1919. Imagining how the city seemed in that year, Mexican author Mauricio Tenorio-Trillo writes in *I Speak of the City: Mexico City at the Turn of the Twentieth Century*:

By 1919 the city must have lost the stink of blood and violence and returned to its natural aromas – horse manure, cilantro, onion, gasoline, flowers, and human excrement . . . the new post-revolutionary buildings and street plans started to emerge. The city was like a stylish and wicked femme fatale just awakening from a long spree of revolutions and abuses, gazing at her disheveled and hungover self: everything to be redone.

This was not the end of the struggle for power in Mexico. One of the main tenets of the constitution was that the president could not stand for re-election, but when in 1920 Carranza put forward one of his close associates as his preferred candidate, General Álvaro Obregón rose against him. Carranza met the same fate as Madero, being shot as he tried to flee the country on the railway to Veracruz. The subsequent election of General Obregón to the presidency in 1920 is often seen as the end of the bloodiest period of the revolution, although political and social turmoil continued for another ten years. (In 1923 the other great peasant leader Pancho Villa was assassinated as he sat in his car.)

It is estimated that between 1910 and 1920 at least a quarter of a million Mexicans had been killed, and as many as three times that number perished due to disease or famine. As in earlier periods of Mexico's turbulent history, tens of thousands of poor people from the impoverished countryside sought shelter in the capital. The revolution also brought intellectuals, writers and politicians from the United States and Europe to Mexico City, curious to see what kind of revolution had been so painfully forged there. Many compared it to the Russian Revolution, and saw in it the possibility of the worldwide triumph of communism. The British novelist D. H. Lawrence visited in 1926 and wrote the novel *The Plumed Serpent* that year, in response. He was troubled by what he saw as the indigenous peoples of Mexico's displacement in the modern world: 'he understands soul, which is of the blood. But spirit, which is superior, and is the quality of our civilization . . . he darkly and barbarically rejects.' At the same time, he had no doubt about who was behind the revolution:

General Carranza with loyalist officers during the 1910 revolution.

Bolshevists, somehow, seem to be born on the railway. Wherever the iron rails run, and passengers are hauled back and forth in railway coaches, there the spirit of rootlessness, of transitoriness, of first and second class in separate compartments, of envy and malice, and of iron and demonish panting engines, seems to bring forth the logical children of materialism, the bolshevists.

The precise ideological thrust of the revolution was to be debated among Mexicans themselves for many years, but when Obregón handed over power peacefully to Plutarco Elías Calles in 1924, it seemed as though the waves of violence of the different factions had finally played themselves out. Calles, though, was determined to further curtail the power of the Catholic Church, and introduced several measures to limit its influence, including banning priests from wearing their robes outside churches. In 1926 he attempted to bring in a nationalized 'Mexican Catholic Church'. This led to disturbances in the capital and elsewhere, and eventually the Catholic bishops suspended all services. When fervent believers began what was known as the Cristero revolt in the countryside, the capital was again spared the worst of the violence, although former President Obregón was shot and killed by a Catholic fanatic in La Bombilla restaurant in the San Ángel neighbourhood. (In 1935 a pyramid was erected in his honour close to the spot where he died on Insurgentes

Sur. It is now at the centre of the Parque de la Bombilla, and has been unkindly described by one Mexican writer as a 'huge Stalinist chimney'. Obregón lost an arm in the battles against Pancho Villa, and as with General Santa Anna's leg, it became a symbol of his resistance to tyranny. For many years it was preserved in formaldehyde inside the monument, before finally being removed and cremated in 1989.)

The conflict between Church and state was to rumble on for several years (as illustrated in Graham Greene's 1940 novel *The Power and the Glory*). Calles, meanwhile, respected the letter of the constitution by stepping down from the presidency at the end of his term in 1928, but he remained the power behind the throne throughout the first half of the 1930s. He was the one who managed the consolidation and institutionalization of the revolution's political and social gains. He also oversaw the spectacular growth of the nation's capital, which by 1925 had a population of more than a million. A new, self-confident nationalism brought with it fresh neighbourhoods, modern styles of building, and a flourishing of the arts and sciences.

7 From Revolution to Megalopolis

One of the main aims of the Mexican revolution had been to prevent a dictator like Porfirio Díaz from remaining in power by manipulating successive elections. The slogan for all levels of Mexican government ever since has been 'Sufragio efectivo, no a la reelección' (Votes that count, no to re-election), a slogan first used in 1910 by Francisco Madero during his election campaign against Díaz. This slogan is even printed on all official stationery, to make sure everyone gets the message. However, this has not meant that the presidential succession has been democratic, as the early years of the 1930s were to demonstrate.

By this time the main political challenge was to bring together all the different revolutionary factions. Under President Calles, the Partido Nacional Revolucionario (National Revolutionary Party) was established in Mexico City early in 1929 to unite all the different sectors of Mexican society. After several name changes, this became the Institutional Revolutionary Party (or PRI, following its Spanish acronym). The PRI was to dominate the political life of Mexico for seven decades, thanks to its ability to accommodate many different groups of society within its ranks. Peasants without land were helped by the creation of *ejidos*, which brought them together to work lands that had previously been exploited by big landowners. Workers were organized in a strong, centralized trade union, the Confederación Regional Obrera Mexicana, or CROM, which pledged allegiance to the government in return for collective bargaining rights and privileges. The PRI also promoted education throughout the country, with primary schooling at least becoming available in many states where there had previously been little or no provision. Education was also made secular, to help encourage a sense of national identity and pride.

This sense of pride was promoted by many revolutionary intellectuals in the capital. Perhaps most prominent among them was José Vasconcelos. As rector of the National Autonomous University (UNAM) based in Mexico City, and then as the head of the newly created Secretariat of Public Education from 1921 to 1924, he argued that Mexicans were 'the cosmic race' because of their rich blend of indigenous and Hispanic heritages. He encouraged painters such as Diego Rivera, José Clemente Orozco and David Siqueiros to paint huge murals on many of the public buildings in the capital, and promoted the publication of cheap books to encourage reading and mass education.

Although Plutarco Calles obeyed the letter of the new constitution and stood down after one term as president in 1928, he continued to be the real power in Mexico under the next two presidents and was known as the *Jefe Máximo* (Supreme Leader) until Lázaro Cárdenas won the presidency in 1934. Cárdenas had served under Calles during the years of revolution, and the *Jefe Máximo* plainly thought he could continue to rule from behind the scenes. Cárdenas, however, had other ideas. He soon sidelined the former president's allies in the central government and the state, and by 1936 Calles was forced to go into exile in the United States.

Cárdenas, meanwhile, was busy taking Mexico in a more radically nationalist direction, closer to his interpretation of its revolutionary ideals. He further strengthened the role of organized labour, and kept the armed forces busy by using troops for major public works projects. But perhaps his most famous move was to nationalize the growing Mexican oil industry. This and other state takeovers, as well as his support for left-wing causes internationally, such as the Republicans in the Spanish Civil War, once again boosted a sense of pride in being Mexican.

This pride was expressed in many areas, from painting and poetry to a wide variety of forms of music. The new opportunities for mass communication offered by the radio and gramophones

The UNAM Central Library building, facade designed by artist Juan O'Gorman.

meant that there was huge public demand for popular songs and tunes. The first radio stations were set up in Mexico City in the 1920s, but it was when Radio XERF 'La Poderosa' began broadcasting in 1931 that the age of radio really began in the Mexican capital. Many of the new stations that sprang up in the thirties either played *ranchero* music that had its roots in the countryside, conveying a nostalgic message for the migrants newly arrived from Mexico's rural regions, or the more exotic Cuban and Caribbean *rumbera* tunes.

Mexican cinema too began to enjoy what became known as its 'golden age'. Mexico had taken to the cinema from its earliest days: the first film was shown in the centre of Mexico in August 1896, only a few months after the first programmes of moving pictures had been put on in France. But it was in the mid-1930s that Mexican film production, based in four studios in the capital, became massively popular not only in Mexico but throughout Latin America, rivalling and often surpassing Hollywood significantly. The film *Vámonos con Pancho Villa* (1936), which mythologized one of the leading figures of the revolution, is widely regarded as the film responsible for starting the upsurge in Mexican cinema production. Over the next two decades, the Mexico City studios produced hundreds of films in many genres, from slapstick comedy to high melodrama and films portraying

A scene from *Los Olvidados* (1950, dir. Luis Buñuel).

serious social concerns. (In this last category, *Los Olvidados*, or *The Young and the Damned*, which was directed in 1950 by exiled Spanish director Luis Buñuel and which focuses on the 'lost' youngsters of the capital's poor neighbourhoods, remains a classic.) There were as many as three hundred cinemas in Mexico City by the end of the 1940s, with hundreds of thousands of ordinary residents faithfully queueing to see home-grown stars such as María Félix and Dolores del Río, and male heart-throbs such as Pedro Infante or Jorge Negrete. Negrete, 'El Charro Cantor' (The Singing Cowboy) was perhaps most famous as the singer of the unofficial Mexican anthem 'México Lindo y Querido' (Beautiful, Beloved Mexico). This ends with the verse: 'Si muero lejos de ti/ que digan que estoy dormido/ y que me traigan aquí.' (If I die far from you/ Say I'm just asleep/ and bring me here.) This was seen as prophetic, as Negrete himself died in Los Angeles at the age of 42, and when his body was brought back to Mexico City for burial tens of thousands of his admirers followed the hearse to the Panteón Jardín cemetery. The day of his death, 5 December, is still marked on Mexican TV and radio with extensive reruns of his most popular films and songs. But possibly even more famous were the two stars of Mexican slapstick of the 1940s and '50s, Mario 'Cantinflas' Moreno and Germán 'Tin Tan' Valdés (who has a small commemorative statue on Calle Genova in the Zona Rosa district). Their humour is so quintessentially Mexican and delivered at such a speed that it often seems impenetrable to outsiders.

Sadly, as in most other big cities throughout the world, the magnificent cinemas built during the 1930s and '40s have now fallen into disrepair, been demolished or been taken over by a variety of religious sects. Perhaps the most striking example is the Cine Orfeón, a glorious Art Deco building in the historic centre able to house as many as 6,000 spectators, which is now an Evangelical Christian temple.

Dolores del Río in the 1945 movie *Las Abandonadas* (The Abandoned, dir. Emilio Fernández).

The tallest triumphal arch in the world.

The Monument to the Revolution

Together with the project for the Palacio de Bellas Artes, General Porfirio Díaz had planned a spectacular new Legislative Assembly building for the centre of Mexico City, close to the new railway stations and the Paseo de la Reforma where it crosses the Plaza de la República. He laid the foundation stone for the ambitious project during the celebrations for the centenary of the fight for independence from Spain in September 1910.

Porfirio Díaz was deposed only a few months later, so that the massive construction remained less than half built, and work on it was suspended. In 1928, the original French architect, Émile Bénard, returned with the idea of turning the structure into a pantheon for revolutionary heroes, but this again came to nothing, and he died soon afterwards. Finally, in 1933 the shell of the original building was reconfigured to create a visible emblem of the revolution in the heart of the city.

The monument consists of an open, copper-covered dome supported on four huge pillars that are some 67 metres (220 ft) high, made of contrasting light-coloured stone and dark volcanic tezontle stone. Sculptures of Independence, the Reform Laws, Agrarian Laws and Labour Laws adorn the top corner of each pillar, while beneath the foot of each column are crypts that contain the remains of revolutionary heroes: Madero, Carranza, Calles, Lázaro Cárdenas and Pancho Villa.

Beneath the monument is the National Museum of the Revolution. This was opened in 1986, and has exhibits relating to the construction of the monument as well as rooms dedicated to Mexican history from the Reform movement in the 1850s to the Cárdenas administration of the mid-1930s.

The Monument to the Revolution has faced the same problem as many of the ambitious architectural projects in the city centre: in the past seventy years the floor of the surrounding square has sunk more than 9 metres (30 ft) into the unstable mud of the former lakebed.

The monument and the museum were cleaned and restored for the independence bicentenary in 2010. A glass-walled lift was installed to take visitors up to the rotunda, from where there are magnificent views of the whole city centre.

By the second half of the 1930s Mexico and Mexico City entered a new era of comparative prosperity, although there were still outbreaks of violence, including an attempt to overthrow Cárdenas in 1938. The increasing power of the central government brought more and more people to the capital: by the mid-1930s its population had grown to 1.5 million. This was also a period of new construction, when the first buildings influenced by the international modernist or functional style began to appear in the capital, and reinforced concrete began to replace stone and brickwork.

Notable examples of this were the headquarters for the electricity workers' union, by the architect Enrique Yáñez from 1938, and that of the cinema industry workers designed by Juan O'Gorman. More importantly perhaps, from the Ministry of Education O'Gorman drove through a campaign for the construction of new primary schools in the capital, all of them designed along functional lines. Many of these are still in use in the twenty-first century. Another radical example of his architectural style was the house-cum-studio that he built for the painter Diego Rivera in the southern district of San Ángel. The new architecture also began to be used for housing projects, in some of the first attempts to cope with the ever-increasing population of the capital.

This was also the period when the first skyscrapers began to appear on the Mexico City skyline, despite the problems created by the dried-out subsoil and the threat of earthquakes. The most emblematic of these was the National Lottery building, designed in 1933, on a prominent corner of the Paseo de la Reforma. It also became known as the Edificio el Moro, as its Art Deco style reminded some of Moorish architecture. For some time its 29 storeys made it the tallest building in Mexico City (until 1956, when the Torre Latinoamericana was built on the edge of the city's historic centre), and it was from here that the first commercial TV broadcasts in Mexico were made in 1950. As with many ambitious architectural projects in the Mexican capital, problems with the soft earth beneath and the threat of earthquakes meant that special engineering solutions had to be found to

The Art Deco National Lottery building.

enable the skyscraper's safe construction, meaning that the 107-metre-high (350-ft) building was finally completed in November 1946. The construction was obviously solid, as the National Lottery building has survived all the recent devastating earthquakes that brought down many nearby buildings. In 2010, as part of the celebrations of the 200th anniversary of Mexican independence, it was carefully restored to its original design, and today it is once again a striking landmark in the city centre.

By the 1940s, the PRI was seen not so much as one political party among several but as the Mexican state itself. Everyone from peasant farmers to factory workers to civil servants was part of the movement, and often owed any advancement to their membership. More left-wing opposition was marginalized (the Mexican Communist Party was banned from 1925 to 1935, and again in 1946) while the grouping on the right, the Partido de Acción Nacional (National Action Party), or PAN, could count on support in the northern states but had little influence elsewhere. Every six years, from the 1930s to the 1990s, a new PRI president was elected. He was chosen by a small group within the party: Mexico was more of a *dedocracia* (the new

The Viaducto Miguel Alemán.

leader was appointed in secret) rather than a democracy. The Second World War (which Mexico eventually joined on the side of the Allies) and its aftermath saw a huge boost in national industry, with many of the new factories being built in the capital or on its outskirts.

The immediate post-war years under President Miguel Alemán Valdés (1946–52) saw annual economic growth of more than 7 per cent. His boast was that he would offer every Mexican 'a Cadillac, a cigar and a ticket to a bullfight', and this economic boom did make some of the capital's inhabitants more prosperous, encouraging still more migration to the capital. As its population grew and grew (in thirty years between 1930 and 1960 it increased more than eightfold) the need for new roads and other urban infrastructure became obvious. In 1950 a brand new multi-lane motorway cutting through the centre of the city, the Viaducto Miguel Alemán, was inaugurated. This was the centrepiece of a large-scale plan to modernize the capital's road system, and was followed in 1952 by the multi-lane Eje Central. Many old colonial buildings were demolished in the crowded streets of the centre to make room for vehicles, but in so doing, according to writer Carlos Monsiváis, this merely created a new chaos:

Eje Central in the borough of Cuahtémoc.

Eje Central [is] a wide road that gobbled up streets formerly known as San Juan de Letrán, Aquiles Serdán, and Santa María la Redonda. This area was considered picturesque; now it looks more like the bastion of the irredeemable: street vendors, stalls peddling food that is as dangerous as urban crime, errant drunks known as *teporochos*, and packs of youths in search of [a] miracle: getting plastered for free. On these streets you can buy any number of horrors. Buyers of the world, behold: pirate videos and tapes, bargain-basement clothing, heaps of socks and T-shirts, perfumes and deodorants, CDs, design-free sweaters, Christmas specials in July . . . People with an air of defeat about them: buyers and sellers are interchangeable (some sell what they don't want to own, others buy what they don't like).

At the same time, Mexico City in the early 1950s burst its bounds and expanded to swallow up the pre-conquest towns surrounding it in the State of Mexico. Between 1950 and 1990, it is estimated that the built-on urban area grew from some 180 square kilometres (70 sq. mi.) to as much as 1,250 square kilometres (480 sq. mi.). Many local residents lament the way in which their city seems to have been sacrificed to traffic. Even so, the municipal authorities have struggled to build enough roads or to organize the capital's transport system in a manner that will keep pace with the rising number of people and vehicles that seek access to the city: it has been estimated that there are some 37 million journeys undertaken on a daily basis.

Just as the city's fabric struggled to cope with this huge population growth, so the PRI found it hard to adapt to a rapidly changing society, where the gap between rich and poor was increasingly wide. As so often in its millenary history, there seemed to be two Mexicos existing side by side: the thrusting, confident modern nation, and the poorer, often rural and indigenous one still rooted in the past. The PRI regime turned to increasingly repressive measures to stay in control. In the capital the cracks in the system became most obvious in 1968, when the city hosted the Olympic Games. This was the first time the Games had been held in Latin America, and the PRI was determined to show the world that Mexico City was a dynamic modern capital that could match Rome or Tokyo, its immediate predecessors as Games hosts. However, the weeks and months prior to the Olympics were marked by student protests similar to those taking place in France and the United States, demanding more political freedom and reforms.

On 2 October 1968 a huge demonstration was held in the Plaza de las Tres Culturas in the northern district of Tlatelolco, near the newly built Foreign Ministry. Although the meeting was taking place peacefully, all of a sudden there were sustained bursts of gunfire, and anywhere between thirty and three hundred people were killed. The government claimed it was the demonstrators who had opened fire on the police, but the student activists said that it was government snipers who began to shoot from nearby tall buildings before the army moved in. Many hundreds were arrested and held for years as political prisoners. Despite the violence, the Olympic Games went ahead as planned, and are now better known for the Black Power salutes given by victorious American athletes than the brutal repression carried out only weeks beforehand.

This repressive atmosphere lasted into the 1970s. Mexico's writers and intellectuals became increasingly frustrated with the PRI's stranglehold on power, and its ability to snuff out criticism and attempts at reform. Although the development of offshore oilfields in the Gulf of Mexico led to an economic boom (which proved to be short-lived) the inequalities in Mexican society, between countryside and city, as well as between the wealthier, more industrialized north and the poor rural states in the south, only intensified. As throughout the centuries, this led to more migration towards the capital.

By the mid-1970s the population of Mexico City had risen to more than 14 million, and the city was sprawling out towards the mountains in the south and the plains to the north. In 1969 the first line of the capital's underground metro system was opened. There are now eleven lines altogether and every day some 5 million passengers are transported in and out of the city. Contemporary authors such as Juan Villoro, in *The Mexico City Reader* have seen the metro as a sign of the split in the capital's population that has persisted over the centuries:

Protest at the Monument to the Revolution in 1968.

bastion of the country's informal economy, hall of exhibitions, concerts, and book fairs, land of sex-cruisers, suicides, and premature births, the metro is a city on the move. The trains are a polished show of imported technology (French-Canadian as it happens), and the modernist design of certain stations is so bizarre that they have been used as sets for science-fiction films ... But it is not the metro's architecture that makes the deepest impression; it's the men and women travelling with expressionless faces, as though they had been bribed to ride it. Mexico City's metro carries five million people a day. Despite their numbers, they have been unerringly selected; to descend the escalator is to cross a line of racial segregation. The underground city is populated by – pick your slur – *nacos*, Indians, Mexicans.

The increase in population has made the problems of everyday life in the metropolis even greater. Air pollution has often brought health crises (breathing difficulties and cardiac failures aggravated by the altitude), and led to schools, factories and offices being closed, especially when the smog lies heavily over the city from February to April. Water pollution has made clean drinking water another area of concern, while the amount of new construction on the unstable, sandy soil has created fresh dangers. As the writer Jorge Ibargüengoitia complained: 'barely thirty years ago, growth was a badge of pride; now it's a terminal disease.' In the end, it was another natural disaster that brought devastation but also positive change not only to the capital but to the whole of Mexico.

Devastation caused by the 1985 earthquake.

8 Apocalypse and Beyond

It was in the early hours of 19 September 1985 that an earthquake measuring 8.1 on the international Richter scale struck the very heart of Mexico City. The damage was tremendous: as many as 10,000 people are estimated to have been killed in a few minutes, and thousands more were made homeless. Hundreds of buildings collapsed entirely, including many famous landmarks in the capital's historic centre, as well as in several residential neighbourhoods. The most tragic collapse was that of the Hospital Juárez, in which more than 560 patients and staff lost their lives. Typically of Mexico, however, what was most reported was that a ward full of newborn babies had survived, even though nearly all of their mothers were killed: these became famous as the 'miracle babies'. Although the city regularly suffers from seismic shocks, this was by far the worst in living memory.

Horror at the scale of the disaster soon gave way to anger when the lack of an adequate response by the local and federal authorities became obvious. Rescue efforts and medical facilities were woeful, lacking direction and coordination. Worse still, many of the buildings that collapsed were recent constructions, supposedly built to withstand seismic tremors. The fact that they did not resist the earthquake pointed to widespread graft and corruption in the building industry and the city government. In an immediate response to the disaster, citizen groups sprang up that often literally took matters into their own hands, digging in the rubble in the search for survivors, or creating temporary shelters and providing clean water and food for the homeless.

Earthquake damage, 1985.

Urban traffic at a standstill.

Anger at the governing PRI and its corrupt ways led to a surge of support for a new leader, Cuauhtémoc Cárdenas, the son of the nationalist president of the 1930s. Although he too came from the PRI, he stood for the 1988 presidential elections as an independent, left-wing candidate. Many Mexicans believe he won the popular vote, but the government announced that the electoral computer system had crashed, and when it was restored, Carlos Salinas from the mainstream of the PRI was declared the winner. This new underhand manoeuvre by the PRI led to further popular protests, while Cárdenas himself helped found the first significant new political party in Mexico for many years. This was the Partido de la Revolución Democrática (Party of the Democratic Revolution, or PRD). The PRD challenged the entrenched position of the PRI from the left with such success that it was widely thought that Cárdenas could win the next election, to be held in 1994.

This election not only showed how far the disintegration of the PRI had gone, but saw a return to political assassinations of the kind not seen since the turbulent 1920s. First the popular PRI candidate Luis Donaldo Colosio was gunned down during an election rally in March 1994. Then in September of that year the president of the party, José Francisco Ruiz Massieu, was shot and killed on the Paseo de la Reforma. In the end, the instability of the political and social climate led to the PRI candidate, Ernesto Zedillo, winning the ballot, while Cárdenas came third, behind the right-wing Partido de Acción Nacional (National Action Party, or PAN). Despite this victory, as the twentieth century drew to a close it was plain that the years of the PRI's dominance were coming to an end. And so it proved: in the year 2000, for the first time in more than seven decades, the opposition PAN won the presidency under Vicente Fox. Since then, Mexico has seen an alternation in government between the PAN and the PRI that has undoubtedly brought greater democracy to the country. This shifting political landscape was confirmed in the July 2018 presidential elections, when Andrés Manuel López Obrador, a former Mexico City mayor who stood as candidate for the recently formed MORENA (Movimiento Regeneración Nacional, or National Regeneration Movement), won a convincing victory over the two main parties.

Mexico City too has seen an expansion of the democratic process in recent years. In 1997 the first election for mayor (or in Spanish, the *jefe de gobierno*) of the capital was held, and was won by Cárdenas and the PRD. Since then, left-wing mayors have led the government of the city from the council building in the historic Zócalo. They have often pursued far more progressive, liberal policies than can be found outside the capital. Unlike many other parts of the country, in the capital abortion has largely been decriminalized. Same-sex marriage was made legal in 2010, and in November 2015 the incumbent mayor Miguel Ángel Mancera signed a decree declaring the capital to be a 'gay-friendly' city. At the same time, although there is a lot of criminal violence in the metropolis, to a large extent it has avoided the bloodshed linked to the trafficking of illegal drugs, as well as the 'war on drugs' declared by President Enrique Calderón (2006–12), which is said to have cost more than 25,000 lives throughout the country.

Direct control by an elected mayor has also resulted in initiatives to improve the city's facilities and infrastructure. By the 1980s, much of the middle class had moved away from the old historic centre out to the periphery, where new blocks of flats and shopping

The Alameda

The park has always been on the edge of the fashionable, polite area of the capital, and the much rougher eastern side of the city. In the 1930s several luxury hotels were built alongside it, perhaps the most famous being the Hotel del Prado. It was in the Del Prado's dining room that in 1947 Diego Rivera painted one of his most famous and enjoyable murals, the *Dream of a Sunday Afternoon in the Alameda*, around 15 metres long and 5 metres high (50 by 16 ft). Under the swaying poplar trees, some 130 figures, almost life-size, are out for their Sunday stroll. Rivera places himself at the centre of the brilliantly coloured fresco, dreaming as a small boy in his breeches and straw boater. He is holding the hand of La Catrina, the cartoon figure of Death, and behind him stands Frida Kahlo. All around him are the figures from Mexican history that people his dreams, from the Mexica Indians to Emiliano Zapata and President Madero, who overthrew Porfirio Díaz.

Alameda Park was at the epicentre of the 1985 earthquake that destroyed many buildings in the centre of the capital. The Hotel del Prado and the other big hotels lining it fell, resulting in hundreds of injuries and deaths.

The Alameda and the surrounding area became home to many hundreds of people who had lost their dwellings. Some inhabited the empty, ruined hotels; others camped out in temporary shelters; thousands of orphaned children lived on the streets. The grassroots organizations that sprang up to provide the aid and support that was lacking from the authorities also chose to make this a Parque de la Solidaridad (Solidarity Park) where they could meet, plan and demonstrate.

Gradually the authorities cleared the site, turning the waste ground into a proper park. Rivera's mural was rescued, pieced together once more and housed in a special museum in one corner of the Alameda Park, where it now draws thousands of visitors every year.

Pathway in Alameda Park.

View of Paseo de la Reforma in the 21st century.

centres proliferated. The congested inner-city areas became increasingly run-down, unsafe and neglected. The destruction brought about by the 1985 earthquake only made the need for renewal all the more urgent.

In response, successive administrations launched ambitious redevelopment plans. Many of these foundered either through political wrangling or the difficulties of aligning the desire to respect the city's rich architectural and social heritage and a wish to improve housing, commerce and transport for the twenty-first century. The most striking of these plans has been the partnership entered into since 2001 between the left-wing city authorities and the wealthiest man in Mexico – and one of the richest in the world – the entrepreneur Carlos Slim.

Slim, the son of immigrants from Lebanon, started to make his fortune with a bottling company and a cement factory, but it has been telephones and the mobile phone revolution that has made him ultra-rich. Keen to demonstrate his patriotism, in the years following the 1985 earthquake he bought up more than 120 properties in the historic centre. In conjunction with the mayor's office, he has undertaken an ambitious restoration scheme that has seen many buildings restored to their former glory, while the streets and public spaces have also been cleaned, and a great effort has been made to discourage the myriad street sellers who used to cram the centre.

As well as this, Slim (whose companies are said to provide some 40 per cent of the total on the Mexico City stock exchange) has been creating a whole new neighbourhood in the north of the city. Officially known as Nuevo Polanco, it is more popularly called 'Ciudad Slim', and contains tall office buildings, outlets for firms such as Saks and Sanborns (both owned by Slim) as well as a huge new aquarium and the Museo Soumaya, so named in honour of Slim's deceased wife.

Since the mid-1980s the population of the federal capital has diminished slightly. This is mainly due to the fact that more people are now living just outside the city boundaries in the sprawling neighbourhoods of the State of Mexico. There are now around 20 million people living in this metropolitan area, roughly one-fifth of Mexico's total population. The capital still acts as a magnet for thousands of

Mexicans from different regions of the country, making it a unique mix of the wide variety of regional cultures and non-Spanish languages spoken in different parts of the country. In addition to all the posts that rely on the highly centralized government ministries and state institutions, the city provides as many as half of the industrial jobs existing in Mexico. As a result, it is no surprise that in 1992 the United Nations declared Mexico City to be the 'most polluted city on the planet'. Fumes from the more than 3 million vehicles in daily use, as well as smoke from factories and seasonal smog, are estimated to be the main cause of more than 1,000 deaths a year.

Further administrative change took place towards the end of 2016. Instead of officially being known as the 'Distrito Federal' (Federal

The aluminium-tiled facade of the Museo Soumaya in Plaza Carso.

Monument of the initials of Mexico City at the Zócalo.

District), the capital has been renamed Ciudad de Mexico, or Mexico City. This means that administratively, the capital is equivalent to the other 31 states in the country of Mexico. The changes are meant to give more control to the local authorities: from now on they will directly choose the metropolitan police chief and attorney general, and the sixteen *delegaciones*, or city boroughs, are to have elected mayors and councils.

In spite of the administrative difficulties and the wearisome problems of daily life in traffic-clogged avenues and streets, often inadequate housing and criminal activity, Mexico City remains an urban centre bursting with energy and creativity. For centuries the scene of natural and political upheavals, the capital city always seems able to re-invent itself, emerging even more vibrant and life-affirming with each shift.

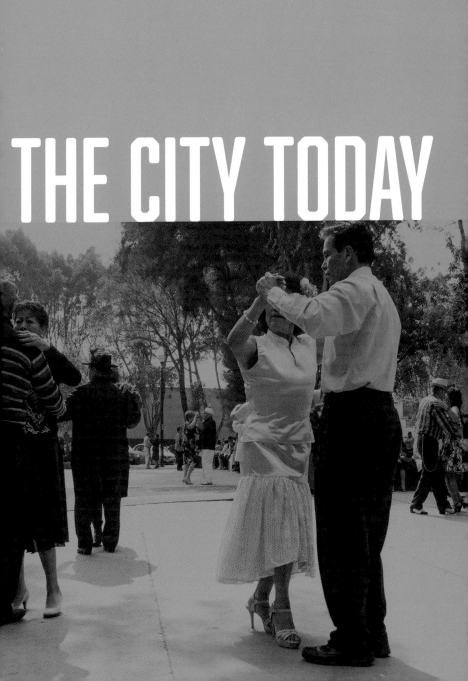

THE CITY TODAY

Lowering the flag in the Zócalo opposite the cathedral.

The Zócalo

At dusk every day, the huge wooden doors of the Palacio Nacional (the National Palace) swing open, and out comes a detachment of soldiers accompanied by a strident brass band. They head for the centre of the square to perform the ceremony of the lowering of the national flag of Mexico (composed of vertical stripes of red, white and green, with the Aztec emblem of an eagle eating a snake on a nopal cactus in the centre). The flag is so large and heavy (it was described by the British writer Patrick Marnham as being 'as big as a tennis court') that the squat soldiers struggle for several minutes before they are able to lay it on the ground and properly fold it up. Then they all march back inside the palace, cymbals crashing and drums sounding.

There can be no mistaking the centre of the Mexican capital. This is the Zócalo, the third-largest square in the world after Moscow's Red Square and Tiananmen Square in Beijing. It is lined on three sides with the buildings that represent the powers in the land: the National Palace, the cathedral with its *sagrario*, or sacristy, and the Mexico City administration offices. On the fourth side nowadays are several hotels built over the traditional Mercaderes arcades. They have rooftop terraces which offer the best views of the square and much of the historic centre of the city, as well as the famous Monte de Piedad, one of the oldest banking institutions in Mexico.

The word *zócalo* itself means a pedestal. In the mid-nineteenth century the Mexican president General Santa Anna wanted a column erected in the middle of the square to commemorate the heroes of the independence battles against Spain. This new monument was to replace the statue of the Spanish king Carlos IV, which then stood on a pedestal in the centre of the square. By the time Santa Anna fell from power in 1848 only the base, or *zócalo*, had been completed, and this gave the square its current name.

The square was at the heart of the city many centuries before Santa Anna decided to site his monument to independence there. This was where the Aztec rulers had their temples and palaces, and where the triumphant Spaniards created their Plaza Mayor, the centre of the new imperial city from which all the chequerboard streets branched out. It was here too that Cortés built an enormous fortress, wary that even though the local indigenous peoples had been subdued by the early 1520s, the Spaniards were still hugely outnumbered and vulnerable. This sprawling fortified palace (occupying four complete blocks with an interior courtyard) was criticized at the time by one official, who claimed that the conquistador was 'building palaces and fortified houses so big that they make up a large village in themselves, and to do so he is using all the towns around Mexico, bringing in great beams of cedar and stone from distant places'.

Following Cortés's downfall, the building was bought by the Spanish crown and became the royal palace; there the viceroys of New Spain resided for the next three centuries. Burnt down during an insurrection in 1692, the palace was immediately rebuilt and cleaned up, and the public market previously housed inside it was closed down. During the 1860s, when the ill-fated Emperor Maximilian I and his wife Carlota made their triumphal entry into Mexico City, they took an immediate and intense dislike to the palace's gloomy interior. It is said that Carlota refused to reside among the heat and squalor of the city centre, and instead insisted that a far more airy residence be built on the crest of Chapultepec Hill. At the same time, the rulers had the Zócalo filled with trees, a bandstand and benches, and designed the Promenade Carlota (soon to become the Paseo de la Reforma) as a wide avenue that would take them from their Chapultepec residence down into the teeming city.

Early in the twentieth century, the seven-times president Porfirio Díaz installed the city's first electricity system in the palace, including an elevator that is reputed to be still in use today. During the turbulent revolutionary years, the palace was bombarded by rebel troops but managed to emerge more or less intact. The obligatory Diego Rivera murals, which the artist worked on between 1929 and 1935, line the staircase. The central space depicts his view of the history of Mexico from the Spanish conquest to the twentieth-century revolution, with portraits of heroes and villainous conquistadores, wealthy landowners and American imperialists. To the right is Rivera's vision of the Edenic world of the Aztecs in the fertile Valley of Mexico, while on the left is his vision of the fruits of the continuing revolution: workers and peasants rise up against capitalist exploitation, under the guidance of a deified Karl Marx.

Throughout the twentieth century the Palacio Nacional was still used for the business of government, and it remains the symbolic seat of power in Mexico, although nowadays the president lives in the official residence of Los Pinos, in Chapultepec. The square in front of the palace is often filled with groups of protestors who camp for weeks or months in sit-ins known as *plantones*, in an attempt to get the attention of their rulers using a method that seems to have changed little over the centuries. The square also attracts throngs of beggars and street vendors selling everything from food to mobile phones. Every so often a municipal decree bans them, and for a while the police chase them away, but they always seem to return. Outside the cathedral there are often groups of dancers performing mock-Aztec rites for the hundreds of tourists who clamour to take selfies in front of the action.

Above the balcony over the main entrance to the national palace hangs the bell that the priest Miguel Hidalgo first rang to declare Mexico's independence from Spain on 16 September 1810 in the small village of Dolores. On the same day each year, the incumbent Mexican president rings the bell and gives the 'grito de Dolores' – the 'shout of Dolores' – to reaffirm the nation's independence. The ceremony always draws huge crowds and is repeated throughout Mexico and in Mexican embassies all over the world.

The Metropolitan Cathedral on the northern side of the Zócalo adjoining the Palacio Nacional took three centuries to complete.

Aztec dancers posing with a tourist.

Jesus as the Lord of Chocolate.

Construction started in the mid-sixteenth century, but it was only finally finished in 1813. Based on the cathedral of Seville in Spain, it is in the shape of a huge Latin cross, with one central and two side aisles, and fourteen chapels along the sides. The Retablo de los Reyes, behind the main altar, dates from the eighteenth century and is perhaps the most interesting artwork on display, along with the statue that depicts Jesus as the Señor del Cacao (the Lord of Chocolate), which is especially revered by Mexico's indigenous groups. A severe fire in 1967 damaged many of the ceiling paintings and several altars, but most of them have been sensitively restored.

But possibly the most striking feature of the cathedral is the way that the floor dips almost as steeply as a ski slope from the high altar down to the body of the cathedral, and the fact that many of its columns are apparently permanently encased in green scaffolding. This is because, as with most of Mexico City, the cathedral was constructed on the sandy bed of one of the former lakes. Over the

Metropolitan Cathedral, view towards the altar showing the sloping floor.

centuries the mammoth weight of the cathedral has led to it sinking several metres – visitors now have to descend steps to enter the building, rather than climb up to it. Even more disturbing is the fact that different parts of the building are subsiding at different rates. This led in the 1990s to the bold decision that instead of trying to prop the whole edifice up, the safest solution was to allow the parts of the floor that were higher to be very gradually brought down to the level of the lowest. This work has been going on for many years now and does appear to have at least stabilized the process.

The same subsidence has affected the cathedral's near neighbour, the *sagrario*. In many ways, this smaller building is more harmonious than its larger neighbour, possibly due to the fact that it was conceived over a much shorter period of time in the eighteenth century, and it is one of the most outstanding examples of Mexican Churrigueresque architecture. Apart from the facade and the artworks, the most remarkable feature of the sacristy is that underneath its foundations it is obvious that the Spaniards built their place of religious devotion right on top of an earlier Aztec temple, with huge wooden

The Metropolitan *sagrario*, or sacristy, adjacent to the cathedral.

beams emerging directly from the still-preserved stone blocks of the Aztec pyramid.

It is not hard to come across examples of the continuing legacy of that pre-Christian era in the Zócalo. Just behind the cathedral and *sagrario*, as a reminder of the city's past before the arrival of the Spaniards, stand the remains of the mighty Aztec Templo Mayor (Great Temple). These were uncovered as recently as the 1970s, and

in the past few years more excavations have revealed that the Aztec ceremonial buildings extend even further than had been thought. One of the most startling recent discoveries has been a 'tower of skulls' in a building next to the temple. The conquistador Andrés de Tapia had described such a place and spoke of the Spaniards' horror at seeing evidence of mass sacrifices carried out by the Aztec priests, but the 2017 discovery of almost seven hundred skulls of not only male warriors but women and children is thought to be the first convincing proof of this practice. In Mexico City, the past is never far from the surface.

Wall of skulls at the Templo Mayor.

Grasshopper at the bottom of the 'Hill of Grasshoppers', Chapultepec.

Chapultepec Park

I f the Zócalo is the centre of power and religion in the Mexican capital, Chapultepec Park in the northwest of the city is where people from all walks of life meet and mingle. Covering over 670 hectares (2½ sq. mi.), it is the largest park in the capital, and draws crowds from all over the city: a recent survey said that more than 10 million people visit it every year. Occupying a wooded hill, Chapultepec offers not only walks among the trees, but three man-made lakes, a zoo, a children's play area, sports facilities, a funfair, restaurants and cafés, and several of the best museums in Mexico City.

Chapultepec Hill (the 'Hill of Grasshoppers' in Nahuatl) is said to be where the wandering Mexica first settled in the Valley of Mexico, early in the fourteenth century. The springs of fresh water on its slopes made it a good place to establish their villages. The Mexica, particularly under their great leader Moctezuma I, planted trees and crops and built temples and palaces around Chapultapec Hill, until they eventually took over areas closer to the lakes in the valley below, and there built their capital Tenochtitlán. Some of the *ahuehuete* trees planted five hundred years ago still survive in today's park, while the remains of the aqueduct that the emperor Moctezuma II had built to supply water to the city down below were recently rediscovered.

During their conquest, Hernán Cortés and his army occupied the hill, tearing down Moctezuma's palace and cutting off the water supply to the Aztec capital below as they laid siege to it. They built a small chapel to San Miguel (Saint Michael) on the summit of the hill, and the area was later used for hunting and bullfights. In the eighteenth century the wooded hill was gradually abandoned, and became known as a hideout for brigands and the poorest members of the booming capital. Following independence from Spain in the early nineteenth century, attempts were made to clear the area, and in 1841 a military barracks was constructed on the top of the hill. This became famous throughout Mexico in 1847, when six cadets from the garrison there are reputed to have leapt to their deaths from the ramparts rather than surrender to the invading U.S. troops. Their heroism is nowadays celebrated in the Altar a la Patria (more commonly known as the Monument to the Boy Heroes) completed in 1952, which marks one of the entrances to Chapultepec Park from the Paseo de la Reforma.

Another more recent monument signalling the entrance to Chapultepec is the so-called Estela de Luz (Pillar of Light). This controversial 104-metre-high (340-ft) column was originally intended as a triumphal arch to commemorate the 2010 bicentenary of Mexico's independence from Spain, and was finally inaugurated in 2012. The delays and huge overspend on its construction, as well as allegations of the misuse of huge amounts of public money, made the Pillar of Light a symbol of the less glorious aspects of contemporary Mexico.

It was the ill-fated Emperor Maximilian I and his wife Carlota who restored Chapultepec's fortunes in the 1860s. Repelled by the heat and confusion of the Zócalo and the historic centre of the city, they had the broad Avenida de la Emperatriz (now the Paseo de la Reforma) built to link the national palace to Chapultepec, and remodelled the Chapultepec military academy to remind them of their love nest Miramare back in Europe.

When he came to power in 1876, Porfirio Díaz made this the official presidential residence, and gradually installed all the latest technological inventions. It was only in the 1930s that President Lázaro Cárdenas had a more sober residence constructed on the western side of Chapultepec, where the Residencia de los Pinos

The 104-m-high Pillar of Light.

remains as the Mexican head of state's official home. The area on this western side of the park is now one of the most exclusive residential areas in the capital. In *Ciudad de Mexico: Espejos del siglo* the writer José Joaquín Blanco has commented acidly on the extravagant styles on display there: 'miniature palaces with monarchical pretensions, like so many mini-Trianons: stained glass, turrets, loggias, balconies, terraces, picket fences, columns, baroque staircases, coats of arms, gargoyles, pediments, friezes, parapets, gardens with their own promenades and benches'.

The Maximilian palace, meanwhile, became the National History Museum (the Museo Nacional de Historia) in 1944. Nowadays lines of schoolchildren and adults make the fifteen-minute climb up to the museum, where the history of Mexico since the arrival of the Spaniards is told through artefacts and temporary exhibitions. On the second floor are rooms left as the emperor and his consort decorated them, while many other exhibition rooms are full of paintings and objects that illustrate the history of Mexico from the Spanish Conquest to the twentieth-century revolution. Of special interest are the paintings done by European travellers in the nineteenth century; and, of course, there are 1930s murals, here executed mainly by José Clemente Orozco, David Alfaro Siqueiros and Juan O'Gorman. Another part of the museum is crammed with historic carriages, including the ornate Italian-made coach that Maximilian and his empress once used to sweep down into the city below.

Works of Siqueiros and Orozco are also to be found in the Museo de Arte Moderno, a 1960s modernist building located just beyond the entrance to the park on Paseo de la Reforma. As well as the muralists, the museum contains works by many other twentieth-century Mexican artists, as well as their nineteenth-century forerunner José María Velasco. More than 3,000 paintings and drawings are on display beneath the museum's glittering golden dome.

North of the modern art museum and across Reforma stands the Museo Rufino Tamayo, built in 1981 and named after the great twentieth-century artist. Here, works by Tamayo form the nucleus of a collection of many Mexican and international painters. Perhaps, though, its most popular feature is the large sculpture court alongside

Mayan temple, an outdoor exhibit at the National Museum of Anthropology.

the building, where giant twentieth-century pieces somehow blend perfectly into their wooded surroundings.

But the pick of the Chapultepec museums, and one that draws millions of visitors each year, is the National Museum of Anthropology (Museo Nacional de Antropología). Housed in a spectacular rect-angular building designed by the architect for the 1968 Mexico City Olympic Games, Pedro Ramírez Vázquez, the museum houses un-rivalled archaeological collections representing different cultures from all over Mexico. Beginning with the arrival of the first peoples into the region, the sculptures and artefacts offer a stunning and comprehensive introduction to the worlds of the Olmecs, the Mayans, the Aztecs and many other indigenous cultures. The centrepiece of the entire collection is the Piedra del Sol (Sun Stone), a five-hundred-year-old Aztec calendar sculpted in a 24-ton circular slab of basalt that is almost 3.6 metres (12 ft) in diameter. Rather than a calendar, archaeologists believe it in fact represents the five eras of the world according to the Aztecs, with the sun god at the centre holding two human hearts in each hand.

Aztec calendar stone at the National Museum of Anthropology.

The upper floor of the museum is devoted to the cultural production of today's indigenous groups, while the shop offers top-class
reproductions of historical pieces as well as original work from
today's artisans.

Close by is another museum devoted to modern art, the Centro
Cultural de Arte Contemporáneo. This belongs to the powerful
media company Televisa, and showcases its extensive collection
of pre-Columbian art, as well as twentieth-century paintings and
temporary travelling exhibitions.

Across the Paseo de la Reforma from this cultural centre stands
the open-air Auditorio Nacional. This amphitheatre has been

remodelled in recent years, and now serves as a venue for concerts, dance and theatre.

Many inhabitants of the Mexican capital come to enjoy the Chapultepec museums for free on Sundays. Others bring a picnic, go boating on one of the lakes, or take their children to the funfair, the zoo or the aquarium. Alternatively, they may watch the dizzying displays of the Voladores de Papantla, who climb to the top of a 30-metre (98-ft) pole and then fling themselves off, attached only by a rope that gradually unfurls until they reach the ground. This spectacular form of bunjee-jumping is thought to date back hundreds of years and is still practised in several states in Mexico.

If visitors to Chapultepec are feeling even more patriotic, they can also visit the Rancho del Charro in the park. Charros are the Mexican cowboys renowned for their huge sombreros; tight-fitting, multi-spangled jackets and trousers; high boots; and jingling spurs. They represent the perfect Mexican macho, as made famous in many of the films produced during the golden age of Mexican cinema, from the mid-1930s to the mid-1950s. *Charrería*, or rodeo, is regarded by many as the national sport of Mexico, and Chapultepec park is where this flavour of the countryside is brought into the heart of the city.

If all this excitement is too much, since 1986 a large area of the park has been known as the Parque de la Tercera Edad (Park of the Third Age), and here more sedate pleasures await. There is a rose garden, a pergola, a library and a pavilion donated by South Korea in honour of the contribution its emigrants have made over the years to bringing the delights of horticulture to the Mexican capital.

Finally, Chapultepec is also home to the Panteón de Dolores, which since the 1870s has been the burial place of many of Mexico's prominent men and women. It is said to be the largest cemetery in Mexico, with more than 1 million people buried here. Many of the tombs are Baroque works of art in their own right, and the Rotonda de las Personas Ilustres (Rotunda of Illustrious Persons), which is home to the graves of three presidents as well as many writers, scientists and artists (including the ubiquitous Siqueiros), is often packed with visitors, especially for the Day of the Dead celebrations each November.

Queuing for *lucha libre* tickets outside the Arena México.

Arena México

It's Friday evening in the heart of Mexico City. A steady stream of people, most poorly dressed but all of them excited, is emerging from Banderas metro station. They are all headed for the Arena México, to enjoy the spectacle of a fight between good and evil, as performed in bouts of *lucha libre*, freestyle wrestling.

By the time the action starts, some 16,000 people, mainly locals, are packed into the cavernous hall of the arena. It was built in 1956, when what some see as a sport, others as art, and still others as pantomime, was at its height, and it was here that the boxing matches for the 1968 Olympic Games were held. Today, it is home to Mexico's most famous three-ring circus, Circo Atayde, and concerts featuring Mexico's top rock and pop bands. But more popular than any of these events is Mexico's particularly acrobatic style of professional wrestling which the 6-by-6-metre ring in the centre of the arena hosts every Tuesday and Friday.

Tonight is even more special than usual, as it marks the 81st anniversary of the introduction of *lucha libre* to Mexico. The main bout will be between two masked men: Atlantis and Arkangel de la Muerte. The wrestlers are preceded by the razzmatazz of scantily dressed young women, strobe lights and pounding music. Once they are in the ring, however, the acrobatic drama of the two bulky masters of the 'pancreatic art' brings cheers and jeers from the huge crowd.

It was in 1933 that *lucha libre* was brought to Mexico from the United States by a former army colonel in the revolution, Salvador Lutteroth. The following year he invited several American wrestlers from the United States to stage exhibition bouts in Mexico. One of them decided to wear a leather mask that covered his entire head, and immediately became famous as *el enmascarado*, the masked one. Ever since, the most popular Mexican wrestlers have all worn masks, to preserve their anonymity and separate their lives outside the ring from the characters they play inside it.

In his groundbreaking study of the Mexican character, *The Labyrinth of Solitude*, the poet Octavio Paz describes Mexicans as always wearing a mask to hide their true emotions: 'The Mexican appears to me to be someone who shuts himself in and preserves himself: his face is a mask, and so is his smile.'

This new sport quickly became immensely popular among ordinary men and women in the capital. Many of them had migrated to Mexico City in search of a better life, only to find that existence in the capital was just as hard as that in the countryside. The elemental struggles performed for them by the wrestlers provided escapism from their own situation as they contemplated the forces of good and evil fighting it out in front of their eyes.

The evil-doer is the *rudo*. He breaks the rules and is willing to stoop to any low in order to defeat the good guy, the *científico* or *técnico*, who displays clean skills and wins by superior strength and ring craft. It is he who always has the crowd on his side. Both wear masks, and the ultimate defeat and dishonour is to have one's mask ripped off, exposing the man (or in more recent times, woman) to the view of all the spectators.

Lucha libre found its first popular hero in El Santo, El Enmascarado de Plata, so-called because he wore a silver costume and a silver mask with teardrop shaped eyes. Born in 1915 as Rodolfo Guzmán Huerta, in the small town of Tulancingo, he moved to Mexico City as a young man and took up wrestling. In 1942 he adopted the persona of El Santo, and for close to forty years after that was never stripped of his mask.

El Santo became the star of many B-movies made in the 1940s during the 'golden age' of Mexican cinema, and he never removed his mask, even when making love to the most voluptuous female agents. According to the film director René Cardona, 'He would

Female *lucha libre* wrestler applying make-up under her mask.

leave the set with the mask still on . . . he ate wearing a mask with a hole for his chin so that he could move his jaw.' In Cardona's films, monstrous women were often the representation of evil, and one particular movie, *Santo en el tesoro de Drácula* (Santo and Dracula's Treasure) was so steamy that he was banned for several years from making films in Mexico.

The Mexican sociologist Carlos Monsiváis described another similar film, *Santo contra las mujeros vampiro* (Santo versus the Vampire Women), as

> a classic of universal kitsch. It demonstrates the viability of the sub-genre and confirms the richness of the ethical struggles being acted out in the ring. While all the wrestling moves and locks are going on, the primordial values of the Universe are revealed through the use of masks, leering eyes, looks that kill,

Souvenir *lucha libre* masks.

clinches, punches that resound in the soul, challenging changes of scene, flying leaps.

El Santo finally retired in 1982, but it was not until two years later, during a TV discussion on *lucha libre*, that he removed his mask and revealed the man beneath. According to the writer Andrew Coe in his book on Mexico City: 'underneath he was humble; bald, with dark bags under his eyes, he looked like a retired worker or craftsman.' But, as all Mexican wrestling fans know, to be stripped of one's mask is to tempt fate. A fortnight later, El Santo succumbed to a fatal heart attack. His mask was replaced in his open coffin, so that thousands of his adoring fans could pay their last respects to their mythical hero.

El Santo began a tradition that proliferated and became the defining feature of Mexican wrestling. Every wrestler wants to have their character and the mask that goes with it. The longer someone can retain their mask without it being snatched off, the greater their fame and the larger the purse for fighting. As in tonight's main bout, when two well-known masked wrestlers are confronting each other, the excitement and tension comes from the knowledge that not only will one of them be defeated, but the vanquished will lose his mask and descend to the level of the ordinary mortal. The wrestler then has to relinquish that character and start all over again with a fresh persona.

However kitsch the wrestling action may seem, and however repetitive the action, *lucha libre* remains second only to football as the most popular sport for Mexicans. It has broadened its appeal in recent years through spectacular tag events, when teams of two or three wrestlers, still divided into evil *rudos* and saintly *técnicos*, do battle both inside and outside the ring. It has also introduced women combatants, who can be as dastardly or angelic as their male counterparts.

The masked heroes who right all wrongs have also spread beyond the confines of the wrestling halls. In 1985, after the Mexico City earthquake, Superbarrio appeared in his superman cape and Mexican mask. His fight this time was against the authorities' corruption and injustices, and for solidarity with the thousands left homeless and without protection. Since then, whenever there is a natural or man-made disaster, many similar figures spring up, offering ordinary people the hope of superhuman intervention on their behalf. In the Arena México the presence of this other dimension is underlined by the ghost of a young girl in a white dress, who is said to haunt the corridors long after the audience and the masked wrestlers have disappeared into the night.

The town hall at Coyoacán.

Coyoacán's Ghosts

Coyoacán is one of the most ancient neighbourhoods in Mexico City, and is a place of many ghosts. Perhaps the earliest of these are the coyotes that gave the pre-Columbian settlement its name, and which can now be admired in the form of a sculpture that depicts a pair of them drinking in a fountain on the main Jardín del Centenario square.

When the Spaniards disembarked in the early sixteenth century, the local Tepanec people welcomed Cortés and his men, and it was from here that he was able to launch his attack on the Aztec capital, Tenochtitlán. After his final victory and the destruction of much of the Aztec capital, Coyoacán was where Cortés established his own palace in 1521, kicking out the indigenous lord who had built it, and settling there with his huge retinue.

The second important ghost to haunt Coyoacán is Cortés's wife, Catalina, who arrived in New Spain unannounced a few months later. Dismayed at the number of mistresses her husband had taken, among them Doña Marina (La Malinche), who had just presented him with a son, Catalina found it hard to adapt to this new life. Within a few months, in fact, she was found dead in her bed one night. Suspicion for her death fell on Cortés himself, who was accused of murdering her because of her complaints. However, one of the foremost historians of that period, Hugh Thomas, concludes that: 'the most probable eventuality is that when Cortés went to Catalina's room, she upbraided him for his mistresses. Perhaps he was nettled, and seized her by the neck . . . at that point Catalina perhaps had a heart attack and died.' In the end, the criminal charge for murder against Cortés was dropped, but it became another item in the long list of grievances that eventually led to his downfall.

It is La Malinche herself who is said to haunt another part of the neighbourhood, around the church of La Concepción, also known as La Conchita because of its intricate Mudéjar facade. According to tradition, this was already a place for worship in pre-Hispanic times, and as elsewhere, Cortés ordered a Christian chapel to be built directly on top of the previous structure. It was here that the first Mass was said in the city, and this is where La Malinche, converted to Christianity, is reputed to have prayed. On one corner of the square in front of the church is the Casa Colorada or Casa de la Malinche, where she is believed to have lived until her death in 1551.

In the twentieth century, Coyoacán is where many of Mexico's most famous artists and thinkers lived and died, occasionally in gruesome circumstances. Foremost among these was the Russian revolutionary Leon Trotsky. Hounded out of Europe by Stalin and his henchmen for his dissident views, Trotsky was welcomed in Mexico by president Lázaro Cárdenas. He was sheltered in Coyoacán at first by the painters Diego Rivera and Frida Kahlo (with whom he apparently had a passionate but short-lived affair) and was later installed in his own house nearby. The house became a magnet for many Mexican intellectuals, and was famously visited by the leader of the French Surrealist group, André Breton, who together with Trotsky and Rivera published the 'Manifesto: Towards a Free Revolutionary Art' in 1938.

But Trotsky's political enemies were still on his trail. In 1940 the painter David Alfaro Siqueiros, a follower of Moscow's hard-line communism, led a machine-gun attack on the house, which Trotsky and his wife escaped by hiding under the furniture. Despite the fact that following this warning a high wall and a watchtower were built to protect the Russian, only a year later the Spanish Stalinist Ramón Mercader broke in and killed the proponent of 'permanent revolution' by driving an ice pick into his skull. Nowadays, the house is a museum and library. The room Trotsky worked in has been left exactly as it was in 1940, down to the pair of small, round glasses on

Frida Kahlo and Diego Rivera in the 1930s.

Inside Kahlo's studio, with paints, wheelchair and easel.

his desk. Trotsky's ashes and those of his wife are buried in a simple tomb in the garden, still much visited by the Trotskyite faithful.

Kahlo herself was born in 1907 and died in 1954 in the house, now known as La Casa Azul, or the Blue House, that she shared with Diego Rivera. Situated on Calle Londres in the Colonia del Carmen area, it was built by Kahlo's father, the photographer Carl Wilhelm Kahlo, as a summer residence, in the days when Coyoacán was still a village outside the limits of Mexico City.

It was here that Frida Kahlo spent many years painting in her bed after a tram accident shattered her spine, and the rooms are still haunted by her presence, with many of the folk artefacts she and her husband Diego Rivera collected. The kitchen walls are lined with *retablos*, the little painted tin plaques originally put up by ordinary people in churches to thank God or a saint for rescuing them from danger or a personal crisis. In the peaceful gardens is one of the

The Casa Azul courtyard.

Trotsky's tomb.

pre-Hispanic pyramids that Diego Rivera built. Few of Rivera or Kahlo's paintings are on display here; most notable perhaps is the unfinished *retablo* 'Self-portrait with Stalin' that Kahlo was working on in the last weeks of her life.

Rivera himself had what looks like a huge, dark mausoleum built only a few kilometres from the Casa Azul. This is the Anahuacalli pyramid, which the artist designed in the 1950s to house his collection of close to 50,000 pre-Hispanic objects. It also contains early studies for several of his mural paintings, including *El hombre controlador del universo* (Man, Controller of the Universe), the final version of which is in the Palacio de Bellas Artes in the city centre. Anahuacalli remained unfinished at Rivera's death, but was completed by his daughter and finally opened in 1964.

One of Coyoacán's more recent ghosts is Octavio Paz, the Nobel Prize-winning poet who was one of Mexico's greatest twentieth-century authors. When his library and much of the rest of his apartment in the centre of Mexico City was destroyed by fire in 1996, he was brought to Coyoacán for the last months of his life, and lived in what was said to be the house of one of Cortés's closest friends, Pedro de Alvarado. Paz died in the house in April 1998, and it was intended that it would become a foundation in his name. A series of disputes meant that this project was never realized, and now the striking red building on Avenida Francisco Sosa is the National Sound Archive (Fonoteca Nacional).

Looking beyond the ghosts, the low-rise buildings made of dark red volcanic tezontle bricks and the narrow, cobbled streets make Coyoacán one of the most picturesque areas of Mexico City. Locals and tourists go there to see and be seen, to visit the craft markets, restaurants, bookshops, cafés and theatres that have replaced the rougher cantinas and pulque bars for which the neighbourhood was famous earlier in the twentieth century, while the colonial church on the Plaza Hidalgo (San Juan Bautista) is a favourite for weddings.

For centuries Coyoacán was a collection of villages separate from the capital, and as elsewhere it is the churches of the area that still act as focal points, although the original parishes have long since been absorbed into the city. Even so, it still preserves perhaps the best collection of buildings from the colonial era, as well as two well-cared-for parks and two main squares: the Jardín Centenario and the Plaza Hidalgo. Both are filled at weekends with crowds of residents and tourists. A Coyoacán inhabitant and habitué at its cafés,

The Fonoteca Nacional.

the writer Guillermo Sheridan has memorably described the people one can find there:

> The scene is a ragbag of home-grown freaks, punks, and aboriginal skinheads mixed in with candy-floss couples, zoom-wielding tourists, legwarmer-wearing pan-flautists, haggard gurus, caramelized socialites ... pomaded spouses, do-gooders with a cause that needs you, and, last but not least, the last of the hippies – *jipis* – still believing in Harry Krishna and talking groovy.

On the north side of Plaza Hidalgo stands the misleadingly named Casa de Cortés. In fact, this was an administrative building in his day and throughout the colonial period, and the current building, still used by the local government, dates from the eighteenth century.

In striking contrast to these ancient buildings is the Viveros de Coyoacán. This is a spacious green area of some 40 hectares (100 ac) created by the city's director of public works Miguel Ángel de Quevedo early in the twentieth century to provide plants and trees for the whole city. It is still used as a plant and tree nursery, but is also a public park, much used by joggers and visitors who come to feed the thousands of squirrels (and the less attractive rats).

Breakfast or brunch: *huevos divorciados*.

A Mexican Breakfast

In the luxury hotels along Paseo de la Reforma and other upmarket areas, the bureaucrats and entrepreneurs hold their first meetings of the day over a meal that can take up to two hours. At the weekends, whole families come out for a treat that is always a boisterous celebration. I head for a small café near the Jardín del Arte, a park where amateur artists gather to sell their daubs on Sunday mornings, just behind the rather glum Monumento a la Madre. It is close to the Paseo, but a very different world from that of the businessmen, politicians and civil servants.

I am always greeted by the owner, 'Claro que sí' – 'Of course you can'. Of course I can sit at any of the tables in this modest sidewalk establishment, walls painted a bilious yellow that somehow manages to blend in with the bright purple walls of the housing block next door. Various *chilango* couples are seated at other tables, all of them intent on their smartphones rather than talking to each other. Talking is difficult anyway, as Mexican hip-hop blares out continuously from fuzzy loudspeakers. The owner speaks good English after living in San Diego for almost a decade, but is pleased that a foreigner is willing to try out Spanish. He (Claro que sí) patiently explains the eggs on the menu: yes, I know *revueltos* are scrambled, *estrellados* are fried, *rancheros* are 'ranch eggs' – whatever that might mean – but what about *divorciados*? Ah, yes, that's two eggs, one with a hot red sauce, the other with a green one. And yes, the sauces are both hot chilli sauces. In case I need more spice, there is a heavy stone bowl containing more of the chillies on the chequered plastic tablecloth in front of me.

In the book *El chile: fruto ancestral*, the writer Paco Ignacio Taibo has helpfully provided an explanation of the difference in meaning between what a Mexican like Claro que sí tells me about the strength of these chillies, and what that might mean for my tongue, throat and digestive system: 'What Mexicans say: It's not spicy at all = It's spicy / A little spicy = Very spicy / Spicy enough = Warning: stay away / Very spicy = Burning hot / Heck it's spicy = Leave the premises while you still can.' Chillies are as essential a part of Mexican identity as chocolate or maize. Many centuries before the arrival of the Spaniards, the indigenous people used them not only as a food, but as medicine and a vital part of religious rituals. Early last century, an American pharmacist by the name of Wilbur Scoville attempted a more scientific gradation of the strength of chillies using what he termed the Scoville Organoleptic Test. This test estimated the amounts of sugared water (in multiples of 100) required to neutralize the effects of different kinds: bell pepper, 0; jalapeño, 2,500–5,000; chiltepin, 100,000–200,000; Habanero, 100,000–445,000. I always settle for the least fiery, with mushrooms or *huitlacoche*, but even so, I need my ration of *frijoles refritos* (refried beans) and several tortillas to calm the inside of my mouth.

The owner clears away the empty plate, but insists I also have the next course: Mexican hot cakes. I see that he is so insistent because, according to one of the banners that are such a feature of life in the Mexican capital, it is hot cake month. These banners seem to be draped on almost every balcony, calling for justice or new housing after the earthquake, or for votes in local elections. 'What is Mexico?' the banner on the wall in front of me asks:

Mexico is greater than any crisis
Mexico is colour, Mexico is tradition
Mexico is the nation of a strong, hard-working race
Mexico is you and me, we are all Mexico
This is an initiative of Mexican eggs and hot cakes
Support Mexico, We are all Mexico!

How could I refuse? Claro que sí strides away, satisfied, and returns only a few minutes later with a pile of hot cakes and the inevitable maple syrup. By now I feel as though I have no intention of moving for at least a couple of hours, but the ritual is not quite finished yet. Claro que sí wants me to round off my meal, as the more refined breakfasters in the nearby hotels do, with a *carajillo*, a strong coffee with a slug of rum in it, to help digestion. Again, I do not have the strength to resist, not even when he offers a refill: 'Claro que sí.'

Once I have finally finished with breakfast, I am strongly tempted to do as the ancient Romans did and regurgitate everything in preparation for the next extended meal at lunchtime – now only a couple of hours away.

Crowd raising Santa Muerte images in Tepito.

La Santa Muerte in Tepito

The sprawling neighbourhood of Tepito is just south of the historic centre of the city, but its thronged streets and cramped one-storey buildings are a far cry from the usual tourist haunts. It is here, on Calle de Alfarería, that the cult of Sacred Death, La Santa Muerte, is at its height.

It was at number 12, Calle de Alfarería, that the first altar to La Santa Muerte is said to have been raised in the city in October 2001, by Doña Enriqueta 'Queta' Romero. Already a follower of the cult, she decided to put her image of Sacred Death on public display, and it is still there, protected by a reinforced glass window. The statue is both striking and gruesome. It is 1.8 metres (6 ft) tall, and is topped with a grinning, white-painted skull wearing a long wig of black hair and what looks like a child's tiara. She is dressed in virginal white, although her robes are changed regularly. At each appearance she is given fresh clothes by devotees who are on a long list of people waiting to show their faith. As with the Niñopa in Xochimilco, she has her day: the 31 October.

But throughout the year, on the last day of each month, the street is swept clean, and other makeshift altars appear in front of the buildings. There thousands of worshippers gather to pray to the figure of Death, to ask for her protection and her blessing.

The followers queue up to pass in front of the image. They cross themselves, bring their own images of the 'saint' for them to receive energy from the 'holy mother' and leave offerings: water, tequila, apples, but also money and flowers. They light candles and often slip their own prayer underneath them for the saint to consider.

A row or two of plastic chairs is set up in the street, to form a kind of barrier to control the crowds, and where mostly elderly or middle-aged women sit to pray to the effigy.

It is already dark when the main ceremony begins at eight o'clock. First the image is purified, usually by one of Doña Queta's family blowing smoke from a cigar onto the skull of the effigy. The ceremony itself is a mixture of a recital of the Christian rosary with more personal prayers addressed to the figure of Death. At the end, Doña Queta or a relative puts one hand on the window of the shrine and invites everyone else to link hands to receive the power and influence of the figure of Death. At another moment, the crowd is asked to hold up all the images they have brought, again to receive the blessing and energy from La Santa Muerte. The ceremony can last for several hours, and as the crowds disperse they are usually offered *atole* maize and rice soup, chocolate and a bread roll.

The cult of La Santa Muerte is said to have developed among the prisoners in jails not only in Mexico's capital but throughout the country, and among the Mexicans held in prisons in the United States. Because their lives were ruled by violence, and death seemed never far away, they began to pray for her (and Death is seen very much as female) protection, accompanied by improvised rituals and pleas for her help. Often, these prisoners had huge, elaborate images of the figure tattooed all over their bodies.

In the past twenty years the cult has spread beyond the jails and begun to attract followers not only among the families of those in prison, but more widely among the working classes, in cities through-out Mexico and especially in the capital. Nowadays, the cult has become a commercial enterprise. Huge crowds gather each month in Calle Alfarería and many other working-class areas of the capital to worship at home-made shrines where the effigies are not of the Virgin Mary or the saints, but Death herself.

This is not a Catholic ritual, and indeed it has been condemned by the church authorities as blasphemous. The 'masses' celebrated in honour of Sacred Death do copy elements of the Catholic service, but there is also a strong sense, as so often in Mexico, that they are following a religious urge that is far more ancient than Christian

Effigies of Santa Muerte.

belief. 'La Flaquita' (the Skinny One) or the 'Niña Blanca' (White Girl) does not tell her followers how to behave or condemn them for sinning. Instead, she listens to their complaints about hardships and injustices they have suffered in their daily lives, and promises to intercede with the Almighty on their behalf. The prayers to her are part confession, part boast.

La Sante Muerte has also become big business. There are statues, adornments, candles, soaps, perfumes and all kinds of images devoted to her. There is even a web page (www.santamuerte.org) offering all kinds of merchandise as well as explanations of the cult.

The cult has spread from the prisons and Tepito to many of the other neighbourhoods in the capital. From the upmarket Colonia Condesa to Villa de Cortés or Dolores, you may come across purple-robed figures that at first look like the Virgin, but on closer examination have the grinning skull of Death. La Santa Muerte also has thousands of followers in the shanty towns on the outskirts of the city, like Ecatepec, and has spread among the Mexican communities living in the big cities of the United States.

As with the medieval figure of Time or the Death card in the tarot pack, the statue often carries in her right hand the scythe with which life is inevitably cut down, and in her left the globe. As more and more ordinary Mexicans feel increasingly unprotected and neglected in their everyday lives, so they turn to the figure of Sacred Death for consolation and a strange kind of hope.

Although Mexico City suffers from the kinds of crime typical of huge cities, and more than three-quarters of its inhabitants see security as a major problem, it has largely been spared the kind of ruthless violence equated with the wars between the large organized drug gangs or cartels. These are mainly run by provincial bosses, and the battles over turf or drug-running facilities take place near the u.s. border or near the coasts of Mexico that serve as staging posts for the trafficking of illegal drugs. However, given the disparities of wealth on display in the capital, and the large numbers of handguns and knives carried by criminals there, as elsewhere in Mexico, tourists need to be careful of which neighbourhoods they visit, especially at night. La Santa Muerte may not protect them.

Los Alebrijes

Giant multicoloured monsters prowl down the centre of the Paseo de la Reforma, heading for the Ángel de la Independencia (Angel of Independence). The procession looks as if the special effects from the *Harry Potter* films have suddenly come to life and are marching through the centre of the Mexican capital. In fact, it is the yearly celebration (near the end of October, around the commemorations for the Day of the Dead) of one of the most original new forms of popular art: *alebrijes monumentales*. The annual parade is organized by the Museo de Arte Popular, but the fantastical monsters themselves originated some eighty years ago through the work of one man, Pedro Linares López.

Pedro Linares inherited his family's tradition of making papier mâché dolls. At first, he made the Judas effigies that were traditionally paraded and burnt when the church bells rang out on Saturday morning in Easter week to celebrate the resurrection of Christ. Fanny Calderón de la Barca, wife of the first Spanish minister to Mexico once Spain recognized the independence of its former colony, provides a graphic description of one of these ceremonies in the 1830s:

> Hundreds of these hideous figures were held above the crowd by men who carried them tied together on long poles. And an ugly misshapen monster they represent the betrayer to have been. When he sold his master for thirty pieces of silver, did he dream that in the lapse of ages his effigies should be held up to the execration of a Mexican mob, of an unknown people in undiscovered countries beyond the seas?

As Fanny Calderón suggests, these Judas burnings could be riotous affairs, and the city authorities have often tried to ban them. In 1957, for example, several dozen people were killed in an explosion in a firework factory in the centre of Mexico City. But the ceremonial immolations have resurfaced in recent years, with the Judas figures today often portrayed as politicians caught up in corruption or other scandals.

Pedro Linares and his family also made the colourful piñatas, the colourful papier mâché or clay balls, with their seven points representing the seven deadly sins, which are a feature of all children's parties throughout Mexico and in many parts of the United States. Their workshops have always been in the heart of the capital, in one of the ancient, narrow streets in the district of Merced Balbuena, just behind the Mercado de Sonora.

Pedro Linares said the idea for these mythical beasts came to him during a serious illness when he was thirty years old. He dreamt he died and was reborn in a mountainous region filled with these

An *alebrijes* parade.

creatures, who called out the word *alebrije* to him. After that, he began to create the beasts he had envisioned, combining at least three elements (tail, body and head) from different beasts – reptiles, birds, insects, dragons and so on – to create a single monster. Their forms are covered with intricate patterns in the strongest possible colours, and each one should be a different, unique creation.

The fame of Pedro Linares's Judases and *alebrijes* began to spread in the 1950s, when he was asked by the artist Diego Rivera to create some huge figures for the imposing black pyramid that houses his collection of pre-Columbian and popular art (the Anahuacalli pyramid in Coyoacán). Linares's work was also prominent in the folk art displays created for the 1968 Olympic Games in Mexico City, and as a result it soon became sought-after by galleries and museums in the United States and throughout the world.

Since his death in 1992, Linares's three sons and his grandchildren have continued the tradition from their workshops in the same street in La Colonia Merced Balbuena. Their work has been copied

Alebrijes on Paseo de la Reforma.

Alebrijes on Paseo de la Reforma.

by many other artists throughout Mexico, with another centre for production of *alebrijes*, in copal wood rather than papier mâché, thriving in the southern state of Oaxaca.

More than two hundred artists now take part in the annual parade organized by the Museo de Arte Popular, which travels from the museum along the Paseo de la Reforma to the Angel of Independence. Several hundred artists take part, as well as groups dressed in costumes. The museum gives three prizes each year for the most imaginative creations. Nowadays, original *alebrije* creations sell for thousands of dollars and are exhibited in museums all over the world.

Pedro Linares originally sold many of his creations in the nearby Mercado de Sonora, part of the vast La Merced market. Opened in

1957 as one of the new public markets intended to regularize street trade in the capital, this huge market is known throughout the city not only for its handicrafts but as the place to buy herbal remedies (*herbolaría*), to ward off the evil eye, and magic potions. Here, for example, you can buy dried rattlesnake, said to help fight cancer, or dried skunk to 'strengthen the blood'.

The magic items include everything required for Santería or La Santa Muerte rituals, from blessed Saint Ignatius Loyola water, said to counteract evil spells, to garlic, horseshoes, magic powders and candles with dozens of different functions. The market attracts thousands of locals and tourists, especially on Saturdays, although the latter are often less keen on another section of the market where live animals, from puppies and kittens to all kinds of snakes and reptiles, are sold from tiny cages.

Rodin sculptures inside the Museo Soumaya.

The Museo Soumaya and Nuevo Polanco

One of the most recent and shiniest additions to Mexico City's art institutions, the Museo Soumaya was built with funds provided by the billionaire businessman Carlos Slim and is owned by the Carlos Slim Foundation. The museum is named in honour of Slim's wife, Soumaya Slim Domit, who died in 1999, and the gleaming curved, ultra-modern exterior was designed by Slim's son-in-law, Fernando Romero. The 46-metres-high (150-ft) building clad with 16,000 hexagonal aluminium tiles has divided local opinion since its inauguration in 2011. Taxi drivers tend to know it as 'the big mushroom', but kindlier architectural critics have praised its boldness and originality. In a move typical of Carlos Slim, the construction company he owns, which manufactures offshore oil rigs, was used to provide the steel columns and beams for the gallery.

The contents of the museum, which extends over six floors of gleaming white space, have also come in for a lot of criticism from art experts. The 66,000 items in the collections on display are heterogeneous, and include everything from Asian ivory sculptures to historical coin collections, Salvador Dalí paintings and a room celebrating the work of the Persian writer Gibran Kahlil Gibran. One of its major attractions is a huge collection of originals and casts by the French sculptor Auguste Rodin, whose work Slim began to collect in the 1980s, and the museum is one of the few places in Mexico showcasing European art from the Renaissance onwards, including works by Tintoretto, Veronese, Andrea del Sarto and many others (although some experts have questioned the authenticity of several of the paintings). There is also a large auditorium that hosts regular lectures and musical performances.

Entrance to the museum is free, and it is claimed that over 1 million people visited it in 2013, making it Mexico City's most popular cultural attraction. The Museo Soumaya is seen as a standard bearer of the new Mexico, in which state involvement in the arts, previously essential for iconic buildings such as the Museo de Bellas Artes or the National Anthropological Museum in Chapultepec Park, is no longer needed, as the private sector can finance more dynamic and less bureaucratic projects.

The museum is part of a much larger development by Carlos Slim called Plaza Carso, but more popularly known as 'Ciudad Slim'. The development contains many outlets of his own businesses, from the department store Saks Fifth Avenue to the restaurant chain Sanborns, a luxury hotel and upmarket apartment buildings. Plaza Carso is said to have cost more than $1 billion so far, but Slim apparently has ambitious plans to extend the scheme still further.

Slim's projects form only part of the ambitious (some say chaotic) recent development of what is known as Nuevo Polanco. In the twentieth century this was a zone of factories and warehouses, just north of the traditionally Jewish neighbourhood of Polanco. Over the past two decades, as industry has moved out of the capital, the old factories have been replaced by luxury residential buildings, office blocks, shopping centres, more museum and art galleries, the 1,500-seat Cervantes Theatre, the capital's largest and most modern aquarium, and other cultural attractions.

Perhaps the most impressive building in Nuevo Polanco apart from the Museo Soumaya is the nearby Museo Jumex. The museum, with its distinctive saw-toothed roof designed by the British architect David Chipperfield, was opened at the end of 2013 to house the contemporary art collection of the Jumex company, one of Mexico's largest fruit juice producers. Jumex also has a gallery on the outskirts of the city at Ecatepec de Morelos, but decided this was too remote to attract many visitors, and so built the new museum. This has become the go-to venue for Mexicans wanting an overview of international contemporary art, with artists as varied as Andy

The Museo Jumex.

Warhol, Jeff Koons, Cy Twombly and Damien Hirst on permanent display, and is known as a place of innovation and experimentation in the arts.

Although Carlos Slim, the Jumex Foundation and others see Nuevo Polanco as the future of Mexico, many others are not so sure. In 2013 further building plans for the new neighbourhood were halted, as the local housing and development authority protested that the estimated population of more than 75,000 was twice what had originally been planned for, creating grave problems for transport and other infrastructural needs. More recently, however, it appears that the developers have won out, with many more new luxury developments crowding in, and others in the pipeline. One of these is the new u.s. Embassy, designed to replace the overcrowded and outdated facility on the Paseo de la Reforma. Announced in 2014, the project has long been delayed due to extensive work needed to clear toxic waste from the site of what was previously the old Colgate-Palmolive factory. Finally, in October 2017 it was announced that the new embassy would be built by a u.s. company using a u.s. architect, while costs have spiralled close to the $1 billion mark.

Boats line the canal at Xochimilco.

Xochimilco

At the weekend, many city dwellers who are keen to escape the noise and traffic of the centre head some 25 kilometres (15.5 mi.) south to visit the ancient town of Xochimilco. Situated at the foot of the Sierra de Ajusco mountain range, this is the capital's last remaining link with the lakes of the original settlements from over a thousand years ago.

The visitors flock to landing stages such as the Embarcadero de Nativitas, where they hire the gaily painted gondolas, or *trajineras*, on which oarsmen will propel them along the waterways of Xochimilco, with whole families eating, drinking and carousing on board. Often, they are accompanied by other gondolas carrying mariachi musicians playing their guitars and trumpets and inevitably singing 'Sobre las Olas' (Over the Waves) or offering a rendition on the giant marimbas of 'Cielito Lindo' (Beautiful Little Sky).

The unique system of *chinampas*, or floating islands that often border these canals, are said to have been founded in the tenth century, long before the local population was conquered by the Aztecs in 1430. These *chinampas* are man-made constructions on the water. Strips of wood are filled with earth and vegetation to create not only fertile plots for cultivation, but platforms for houses.

By the time the Spaniards arrived in the early sixteenth century, Xochimilco was famous for supplying the inhabitants of the Aztec capital, Tenochtitlán, with flowers, fruits and vegetables: the fertile black soil could produce three or four harvests a year. This tradition continued throughout the colonial period, and it was only in the second half of the nineteenth century that Xochimilco began to become a destination for city dwellers looking to get out into the fresh air and picnic on its 170 kilometres (105 mi.) of canals and lakes. It was then too that its waters began to be used to supply the capital with fresh water, along a 27-kilometres (17-mi.) aqueduct to Condesa in the heart of the city.

During the years of revolution after 1910, Xochimilco suffered from the violence like much of the capital, but its most famous moment came in 1914 when the two guerrilla leaders, Pancho Villa from the north and Emiliano Zapata from the south, agreed to join forces against the government and signed the Pacto de Xochimilco.

Throughout the twentieth century the pressures on the natural and man-made beauties of Xochimilco have only increased. The growth of urban sprawl has meant that the area's population is now close to half a million, with housing developments and illegal settlements increasingly encroaching on the traditional smallholdings and market gardens.

This population increase, the overuse of water resources and overexploitation of other natural resources have put a great strain on the centuries-old ecosystem. The freshwater springs have almost been

Laundresses at Xochimilco, 1900.

exhausted, and the lowering of the water table means that the canals could dry out. In addition, some years ago water hyacinths were introduced in an attempt to cleanse the waters. Unfortunately, these plants grew out of control and now block many of the waterways, but renewed efforts have been made to enforce strict environmental safeguards that protect the remaining few.

On land, many places sell all kinds of *helado*, or ice cream (another ancient tradition from the days when ice from the nearby sierras was flavoured and sold in Xochimilco). Nowadays, street sellers offer flavours from pulque to rose petal, especially during the festival at Santiago Tulyehualco every April. Elsewhere, the fruit and vegetable and houseplant *tianguis*, or markets, also continue to thrive, and are at their most colourful in the days before Christmas, when thousands of *flores de Pascua* (poinsettia plants) are laid out on display.

It is also in the run-up to Christmas that one of Xochimilco's best-known traditions reaches its climax. The Spaniards built several fine churches in Xochimilco, which became part of the lands ceded to the conquistador Pedro de Alvarado. Among them are the Capilla del Rosario, with its Moorish tiles, and the Franciscan convent of San Bernardino of Siena, which was completed in 1590. The church has a sober, even austere facade, but inside there are soaring 24-carat gold-leaf *retablos* that are as fine as any in the city. The patron saint of the church is a statue some 50 centimetres (20 in.) high of the infant Jesus, known as the Niñopa (Nahuatl for 'child of this place'). This little figure has been credited with many miracles over the centuries. It is said that his tiny shoes get worn out because of all the visits he makes to the homes of the sick and destitute.

Niñopa's saint's day is 2 February, and each year the statue is placed under the protection of a single family, the *mayordomos*, who have to look after him and shower him with gifts for that year. So strong is the tradition that there is a waiting list of some forty or fifty years for the honour of housing the statue. Although the faithful can come and pray and bring him gifts throughout the year, it is during the nine days of the *posadas* before Christmas that this worship reaches its climax, with thousands crowding into the family's home to receive the child's blessing.

The Niñopa shrine in the Capilla del Rosario.

It is also in Xochimilco that some of the finest works by the painters Diego Rivera and Frida Kahlo can be seen. They are housed in the park of a seventeenth-century hacienda purchased towards the end of the last century by the rich businesswoman Dolores Olmedo, who died in 2002. A patron of Rivera's, she acquired many of his oil paintings, watercolours and lithographs. More than a hundred, together with forty works by Frida Kahlo, are now on display to the public in an airy, well-designed museum that also contains her collection of pre-Hispanic objects and folk art. In the park outside strut proud peacocks, and there are also roaming xoloitzcuintin, a hairless breed of dog that dates, like Xochimilco itself, back to pre-Hispanic days.

The canals are lined with a kind of juniper tree known as the *ahuejote*, which thrives in shallow water and supports a huge variety of aquatic wildlife. Pride of place must go to the axolotl, the fiercely ugly amphibian that is native to Xochimilco and is at home either underwater or on land, as it breathes through both gills and lungs. By the second decade of this century, it was thought that only some five hundred of these unique creatures still survived in the wild. Like much of Xochimilco, which was declared a UNESCO World Heritage Site in 1987, the threat of its disappearance is far too real.

Children on a pilgrimage to the Virgen de Guadalupe.

Virgen de Guadalupe

On 12 December each year, several million pilgrims make their way to the basilica on Tepeyac Hill, which is dedicated to the shrine of the Virgen de Guadalupe (Virgin of Guadalupe). When the Spaniards conquered the Aztecs early in the sixteenth century, they did so in the name not only of the Spanish emperor Charles v, but of the Christian religion. But although they replaced the indigenous temples with churches and monasteries and preached the gospel, there remained some doubt as to whether the power of Christ was directly in evidence on the new continent.

Any such doubt was removed when, according to legend, a local farmer by the name of Cuauhtlatohuac, baptized with the name of Juan Diego, was walking down Tepeyac Hill to the north of the city when the Virgin Mary suddenly appeared to him 'radiant as the sun, with the rock glowing like jewels beneath her feet'. She called on him to persuade the bishop of Mexico City to build a church in her name on the hillside, a church that would above all be for the indigenous Mexicans, as 'I am the mother of all of you who dwell in this land.'

The bishop at first refused to believe in the apparition. He called on Juan Diego to provide concrete proof of her appearance. Over the next couple of days, Juan Diego was kept busy looking after a dying uncle. When he returned to Tepeyac on 12 December 1531, the Virgin appeared to Juan once more. In one of the most famous phrases in the Mexican Christian tradition, she asked him, 'No estoy yo aquí, que soy tu madre?' (Am I not here, I who am your mother?) and told him to return to the first place where he had seen her. There

The pilgrimage to the basilica on Tepeyac Hill.

he found a Spanish rose bush in bloom out of season on the barren, volcanic hillside. Gathering the roses in his cloak, Juan Diego rushed down to the bishop's palace, where he poured out the petals in front of the dignitary. When the cloak was emptied, the figure of a dark-skinned indigenous Virgin was seen imprinted on the cloth. Not only that, but Juan Diego's uncle had made a miraculous recovery.

A chapel was soon built on the hill to house the miraculous cloak, known as the *tilma*. The shrine was known as the Virgin of Guadalupe in honour of the Black Madonna venerated back in Extremadura in Spain, the birthplace of many of the original conquistadores. The Virgin became known as *Tonantzin*, or 'our little mother', and over the years, many miracles have been attributed to the holy image, which has remained the most popular Christian image among the local *mestizo* population. At first, the Catholic Church hierarchy shared the bishop's scepticism. They were also concerned that the religious fervour of the *mestizos* might be an indication that they were continuing to worship their pre-Christian deities concealed beneath the new practices – there had been a temple here long before the Spaniards set foot in Mexico, and the sulphur springs at the foot of the hill were said to have magical healing powers. Over the years, however, the Virgin gained acceptance among the Church author-ities, and became the patron saint not only of Mexico City but of all Latin America. And in May 1990, during a mass held by Pope John Paul II at the basilica, Juan Diego himself was declared a saint.

Nowadays not a day goes by without different processions head-ing up the hill. They may be members of a trade union, or a cycling club, or parishioners from a church anywhere in Mexico. Many of the most fervent believers crawl the last 3 kilometres (2 mi.) on their knees to fulfil their 'promise' to the Virgin for having delivered them from some personal crisis. The main church building now dates from

Pilgrim with the Virgin's icon.

1976, and is a huge, unlovely concrete structure that has little of the grace of its predecessors. Inside there is a circle of pews that can accommodate up to 20,000 worshippers, with the original image of the Virgin displayed on a huge frame behind a bullet-proof glass screen above the main altar. A travelator takes the faithful along behind the sacred cloth, and out onto the promenade.

Above the new basilica the old Baroque church from the end of the seventeenth century, which earthquakes and subsidence have made unsafe, is now a religious museum. Further up Tepeyac Hill are the Iglesia del Cerrito and the Capilla del Pocito, a circular chapel with three blue-and-white domes built around a deep well.

Virgen de Guadalupe votives, icons and bouquets.

Pilgrims enter the basilica of the Virgen de Guadalupe.

Two stairways lead from here to the summit of the hill, where the pre-Columbian temple to Tonantzín stood many hundreds of years ago. From high up here, pollution permitting, the vast city can be seen stretching out to the southern horizon.

The English Catholic novelist Graham Greene described the scene in the late 1930s in his travel book *The Lawless Roads*, and it still gives a good impression of the throng around the shrine:

> Afterwards we climbed up the steep winding stairs which go up Tepeyac hill behind the shrine, to the chapel built on the spot where the Virgin first appeared. At every corner photographers stood with their old hooded cameras on stilts and their antique screens – an early steamship, a train, a balloon, improbable aeroplanes out of Jules Verne, and of course the swans and lakes, blue Danubes and roses, of that nostalgic period. Little braziers burned, and there was a smell of corncake all the way up. Near the chapel is the rich man's cemetery, huge tombs with Spanish

coats of arms of lichened stone, huddling for safety near the peasants' shrine. There is no earth on Tepeyac hill; it has to be carried up by human labour, and every grave must be drilled out of the solid rock.

LISTINGS

Hotels

St Regis Mexico City
Avenida Paseo de La Reforma 439, Cuauhtémoc, 06500
+ 52 55 5228 1818
www.stregismexicocity.com
One of the newest luxury hotels in the city, the St Regis is a 31-storey tower in a prime spot on Reforma Avenue.

Four Seasons Mexico City
Avenida Paseo de La Reforma 500, Juárez, 06600
+52 55 5230 1818
www.fourseasons.com/mexico
The place to have a long, slow Mexican breakfast.

Gran Hotel Ciudad de México
Avenida 16 de Septiembre 82, Centro, 06000
+52 55 1083 7700
www.granhoteldelaciudaddemexico.com.mx/en
Situated just off the Zócalo, this Art Deco hotel has a magnificent roof terrace overlooking the main square.

Hotel Habita
Avenida Presidente Masaryk 201, Polanco, 11560
+52 55 5282 3100
www.hotelhabita.com
A popular hipster hangout with contemporary art on display and an infinity pool on the roof.

Hotel Villa Condesa
Calle Colima 428, Roma Norte, 06700
+ 52 55 5350 9592
www.villacondesa.com.mx/en-gb
A reasonably priced hotel in the historic centre of the city.

Emporio Reforma

Avenida Paseo de La Reforma 124, Juárez, 06600

+52 55 5351 6906

www.emporiohotels.com/hoteles/emporio-mexico-city

Situated on Avenida de la Reforma, this relatively modest hotel is favoured by Mexicans.

Casa San Ildefonso

Calle San Ildefonso 38, Cuauhtémoc, 06000

+52 55 2616 1657

www.casasanildefonso.com

A very central, inexpensive hostel in the heart of the city.

Casa Jacinta Guest House

Segunda Cerrada de Belisario Domínguez 22, Coyoacán, 04100

+52 55 7098 9384

www.casajacintamexico.com/en

A homely guest house conveniently situated near the Frida Kahlo 'Blue House' in Coyoacán.

The Red Tree House

Calle Culiacan 6, Condesa, 06100

+52 55 5584 3829

www.theredtreehouse.com

Situated on a quiet street in residential Colonia Condesa, this guest house offers bed and breakfast in a 1920s Art Deco building.

Hotel Carlota

Calle Rio Amazonas 73, Cuauhtémoc, 06500

+52 55 5511 6300

www.hotelcarlota.com.mx/en

A recently refurbished boutique hotel with a central swimming pool and walls decorated with contemporary artwork.

Bars and Cantinas

Licorería Limantour
Avenida Álvaro Obregón 106, Roma Norte, 06700
http://limantour.tv/eng
This contemporary cocktail bar has been judged to be among the world's fifty best bars every year since 2014.

Cantina El Tío Pepe
Avenida Independencia 26, Centro, 06050
This traditional cantina first opened in 1870 and has kept its Art Nouveau decor.

Pulquería Los Insurgentes
Avenida Insurgentes Sur 226, Roma Norte, 06700
Los Insurgentes is a four-storey building devoted to the consumption of pulque, the once-again popular Mexican drink made from the agave plant.

Las Duelistas
Aranda 28, Centro, 06400
A traditional bar serving pulque, Las Duelistas is now favoured by the hipster brigade.

Café La Habana
Avenida Morelos 62, Juárez, 06600
This coffee house is famous as the place where Fidel Castro and Che Guevara met to plan the Cuban Revolution.

Bookshops

For the widest array of literary books in Mexico City, try the Librerías Gandhi. The original bookshop is at Miguel Angel de Quevedo 121, Coyoacán, but there are now seventeen branches across the city.

El Péndulo
Calle Alejandro Dumas 81, Polanco, 11560
A pendulum reminds visitors of the passing of time in this Polanco bookshop, which also boasts a fine café. (El Péndulo also has branches in the La Condesa and Roma neighbourhoods.)

Librería Rosario Castellanos
Tamaulipas 202, Condesa, 06170
www.fondodeculturaeconomica.com
Also known as the Centro Cultural Bella Época – as it includes a cinema and art gallery – this is the place to find books from Mexican state-supported publishing houses.

Centro Cultural Elena Garro
Calle Fernández Leal 43, Coyoacán, 04020
www.educal.com.mx/elenagarro
Situated in the traditional neighbourhood of Coyoacán, this bookshop (named in honour of the poet Octavio Paz's first wife) specializes in children's books from all over the world.

Un lugar de la Mancha
Esopo 11, Chapultepec Morales, 11570
www.lamancha.com.mx
This independent bookshop has a good café and sometimes hosts cultural events.

Cafés and Restaurants

Alelí
Calle Sinaloa 141, Roma Norte, 06700
+52 55 2124 4590
Alelí serves regional cuisine from all over Mexico in a relaxed atmosphere.

Amaya
General Prim 95, Juárez, 06600
+52 55 5592 5571
www.amayamexico.com
This famous wine bar has small, inviting rooms that are ideal for intimate occasions.

La Docena
Avenida Álvaro Obregón 31, Roma Norte, 06700
+ 52 55 5208 0833
www.ladocena.com.mx
Oysters, shrimp, ceviche and other fine seafood are served in this cosmopolitan bar that is a popular drinking spot among the city's fashionistas.

El Moro
Eje Central Lázaro Cárdenas 42, Centro, 06000
+52 55 5512 0896
www.elmoro.mx
This central café has been in business since 1935 and is still the place to go for a breakfast of Mexican hot chocolate and fried churros.

Pujol
Calle Tennyson 133, Polanco, 11570
+52 55 5545 4111
www.pujol.com.mx
Regularly voted among the world's top fifty restaurants, Pujol has moved to brand-new premises but still serves the same superlative food.

Rosetta

Calle Colima 166, Roma Norte, 06700

+52 55 5533 7804

www.rosetta.com.mx

Run by Elena Reygadas, winner of the 2014 Prize for Latin America's Best Female Chef, this distinctive restaurant focuses on seasonal Mexican produce.

Taquería los Parados

Monterrey 333 (on the corner of Baja California), Roma Sur, 06760

+52 55 5264 7138

This low-key taqueria serves tacos with all kinds of grilled meat, exciting salsas and *cazuelas*, to be eaten while standing at the counter.

Don Toribio

Bolívar 31, Centro, 06000

+52 55 5510 9198

Grilled meats, Mexican breakfasts and other typical Mexican dishes are served here in what is said to be the best budget restaurant in the city centre.

Raíz cocina de estaciones

Schiller 331, Polanco, 11560

+52 55 5250 0274

As the name suggests, this restaurant offers a menu of modern Mexican dishes and local produce that changes in accordance with the seasons.

Café de Tacuba

Calle de Tacuba 28, Centro, 06010

+52 55 5521 2048

www.cafedetacuba.com.mx/en

Situated in a former seventeenth-century convent, this traditional café/restaurant in the historic centre serves many authentic Mexican dishes.

Dancing and Live Music Venues

California Dancing Club
Calzada de Tlalpan 1189, San Simón, 03660
+52 55 5539 3631
This popular club is known as the temple for live Latin music in Mexico City.

Kimbara
Calle Francisco Pimentel 78, San Rafael, 06470
+52 55 8531 2838
A new venue where locals meet to dance salsa.

Mama Rumba
Calle Querétaro 230, Roma Norte, 06700
+52 55 5564 6920
 Mama Rumba offers mojitos, Caribbean food and Cuban music.

Salón Calavera
Calle de Tacuba 64, Centro, 06210
+52 55 5512 5402
The place for reggae and other Latin roots music.

Salón Los Ángeles
Calle de Lerdo 206, Guerrero, 06300
+52 55 5597 5181
The oldest dance hall in Mexico City, Salón Los Ángeles opened in 1927 and is still going strong.

San Luis Club
Calle San Luis Potosi 26, Cuauhtemoc, Roma Sur, 06700 Ciudad de México
+52 55 5574 2639
A retro dance venue where professional dancers mingle with millennial hipsters.

Markets

La Ciudadela
Avenida Balderas, Centro, 06040
www.laciudadela.com.mx
Situated next to an old fortress, this is the largest handicrafts market in the city centre.

La Lagunilla
Metro Garibaldi, Centro, 06020
A genuine flea market operating every Sunday in the heart of the historic city centre.

Mercado de Coyoacán
Centro de Coyoacán, Hidalgo and Malitzin, 04100
www.centrodecoyoacan.mx
This market specializing in food and arts and crafts is crowded with locals and tourists every weekend.

La Merced
Calle Rosario, Merced Balbuena, 15810
This is the most traditional market in the city. Locals come here to shop for vegetables, meat, fish and cheese, as well as to eat at the numerous food stalls, which serve amazing treats at great prices.

Mercado de Sonora
Fray Servando Teresa de Mier 419, Merced Balbuena, 15800
A traditional market where it's possible to buy anything from herbs and spices to love potions and even live animals.

Mercado Roma
Calle Querétaro 225, Cuauhtémoc, Roma Norte, 06700
Foodies descend on Mercado Roma to sample the latest food trends, from tacos to *helado*.

Art Galleries

Proyectos Monclova
Calle Colima 55, Roma Norte, 06700
+52 55 5525 9715
www.proyectosmonclova.com/en
Housed in a converted pool hall, this gallery shows both Mexican and international art.

Kurimanzutto
Gob. Rafael Rebollar 94, Miguel Hidalgo, San Miguel Chapultepec, 11850
+52 55 5256 2408
www.kurimanzutto.com/en
Established in the late 1990s, Kurimanzutto is known for promoting work by contemporary Mexican artists.

Galería OMR
Calle Córdoba 100, Roma Norte, 06700
+52 55 5207 1080
www.galeriaomr.com
This is one of the most established of Mexico City's contemporary art galleries, situated in the hip Roma Norte district.

Museo Frida Kahlo
Calle Londres 247, Coyoacán, 04100
+52 55 5554 5999
www.museofridakahlo.org.mx
The Casa Azul, or Blue House, is where Frida Kahlo, one of Mexico's best-known twentieth-century artists, lived and worked for many years.

Museo Nacional de Arte (MUNAL)
Calle Tacuba 8, Cuauhtemoc, Centro, 06010
www.munal.mx/en
Located in the middle of the historic centre, close to the Palacio de Bellas Artes, MUNAL shows a collection of Mexican art produced between the late sixteenth and mid-twentieth centuries.

Museo Jumex

Miguel de Cervantes Saavedra 303, Granada, 11520

+52 55 5395 2618

www.fundacionjumex.org/en

The so-called MOMA of Mexico City, the five-storey Museo Jumex shows works by contemporary artists such as Gabriel Orozco, Jeff Koons and Andy Warhol.

Museo Universitario Arte Contemporáneo (MUAC)

Insurgentes Sur 3000, Coyoacán, 04510

+52 55 5622 6972

www.muac.unam.mx

Showing works from the second half of the twentieth century onwards, the gallery is situated in a highly distinctive building in the southern district of Coyoacán.

Museums

Museo Nacional de Antropología

Paseo de la Reforma and Calzada Gandhi, Polanco, 11560

www.mna.inah.gob.mx

Housed in a stunning building designed in 1964, the National Museum of Anthropology has extensive displays of sculptures and artefacts from all the classical civilizations of Mexico.

Museo Dolores Olmedo

Avenida México 5843, La Noria, 16030

www.museodoloresolmedo.org.mx

This eighteenth-century estate, owned by the collector Dolores Olmedo, houses the world's largest collection of Frida Kahlo paintings, as well as many by her husband Diego Rivera and their contemporaries. The grounds of the property are also spectacular.

Museo de Arte Popular (MAP)

Revillagigedo 11, Centro, 06050

www.map.cdmx.gob.mx

A vibrant celebration of handicrafts from all over Mexico housed across several floors in an Art Nouveau palace.

Museo Soumaya

Boulevard Miguel de Cervantes Saavedra 303, Miguel Hidalgo, 11529

www.museosoumaya.org

The museum, named for the deceased wife of businessman Carlos Slim, houses his private and eclectic art collection, including the second-largest collection of Auguste Rodin pieces in the world.

Shopping

Antara Fashion Hall

Avenida Ejercito Nacional Mexicano 843, Miguel Hidalgo, 11520

www.antara.com.mx

A modern shopping centre with international designer outlets and a large food hall.

Centro Santa Fe

Prolongacion Vasco de Quiroga 3800, Contadero, 05500

www.centrosantafe.com.mx

An ice rink adds to the attractions in this recently expanded shopping centre.

El Palacio de Hierro

Avenida Moliere 222, Polanco, 11530

www.elpalaciodehierro.com

This is a new Nuevo Polanco branch of a traditional department store, comprising Mexican and international outlets.

Perisur

Anillo Periférico Sur 4690 Coyoacán, 04500

www.galerias.com/Perisur

Located on the southern ring road, this upmarket shopping centre is one of the most popular department stores in the city. It is renowned for its extravagant Christmas displays and its twenty-screen cinema.

Reforma 222

Avenida Paseo de la Reforma 222, Juárez, 06600

www.codigoreforma222.com.mx

A glass-covered shopping centre spread over four floors and located on one of Mexico City's most fashionable avenues.

Sights

Antiguo Colegio de San Ildefonso

Justo Sierra 16, Centro, 06020

www.sanildefonso.org.mx

Located in the city centre, this colonial palace was one of the main seats of learning from the early days of the Spanish conquest until the mid-twentieth century. The Baroque exterior is matched by the ceilings and stonework inside, and the interior is decorated with the inevitable murals by Rivera and co.

Cabeza de Juárez

Avenida Guelatao, Iztapalapa, 09227

This huge 13 by 9 metre (43 by 30 ft) statue of Mexico's first indigenous president, Benito Juárez, is in Iztapalapa on the road out to the east of the city. Originally designed by Siqueiros in 1972 for the anniversary of the nineteenth-century hero's death, it was completed after his own death in 1976. A museum outlining the president's life and achievements was added in the year 2000. The sculpture's crude depiction of Juárez, stressing his indigenous features, has made the statue controversial, and the site is better known by many local residents for being next to the main city car pound for towed-away vehicles.

Ciudad Universitaria

Avenida Universidad 3000, Coyoacán, 04510

www.unam.mx

This vast campus is home to one of the world's biggest universities. It also houses the stadium that was used for main events in the 1968 Summer Olympics, several museums and the famous central library, which has exterior decoration by Juan O'Gorman.

Casa de los Azulejos

Avenue Francisco Madero 4, Centro, 06500

With its tile-covered facade, this eighteenth-century palace is one of the most striking buildings from the Spanish Viceregal period. Its covered patio now houses a Sanborn's restaurant, which is a favourite spot for business and tourist breakfasts.

Plaza Garibaldi

Eje Central Lázaro Cárdenas, Centro, 06010

Plaza Garibaldi is known as a great spot for watching typical mariachi bands in all their finery. Venues range from the very traditional to the most touristy.

Desierto de los Leones

Cuajimalpa/Álvaro Obregón

Covering almost 2,000 hectares (5,000 acres), the Desierto de los Leones is a national park within the limits of the city. It has forests of pines and holm oaks, waterfalls and ravines, and is the oldest protected biosphere in Mexico.

Parque hundido

Avenida Insurgentes Sur, Extremadura Insurgentes, 03740

This traditional park in the south of the city features impressive reproductions of sculptures from the many different classical Mexican cultures.

Chronology

12000 BC	The first settlements appear around the lakes of the Valley of Mexico
100 BC	The rise of the city of Teotihuacán. Various small towns trade and feud around the lakes
c. AD 700	The fall of the city of Teotihuacán
1325	Tenochtitlán, the Aztec capital, is founded
1502	Moctezuma II becomes Aztec emperor
1519	On 8 November, Hernán Cortés and his army enter Tenocthitlán and are at first warmly received by Moctezuma
1520	On 1 July, the 'Night of Sorrows', Cortés and the Spaniards are driven from the city
1521	Cortés wins his final victory over Moctezuma and the Aztecs; Moctezuma is killed. In October the first Spanish municipality of Coyoacán is founded
1527	The first *audiencia* of New Spain is created and Cortés is stripped of power and summoned back to Spain in 1528
1535	Charles V appoints the first Viceroy of New Spain, Antonio de Mendoza
1539	The first printing press is established. For many years it remains the only one throughout the Spanish empire in the Americas
1551	The Royal and Pontifical University of Mexico is founded

1604   Bernardo de Balbuena's epic poem on Mexico City, *Grandeza Mexicana*, is published

1607   Crown officials make the first attempts to drain the lakes in order to prevent flooding in the capital

1629   A great flood almost leads to abandonment of the city

1692   There is widespread revolt in the city against Spanish rule

1722   The first Mexican newspaper, *La Gaceta de México*, is published

1810   Revolutionary forces led by Father Miguel Hidalgo reach close to Mexico City but turn back

1821   Agustín de Iturbide enters Mexico City and Mexican independence is declared

1824   The first constitution of independent Mexico is passed. Mexico City is made the federal capital

1838   The 'Pastry War' with France begins after a French bakery in Mexico City is attacked

1847   U.S. troops attack the military academy on Chapultepec Hill, defended by the cadets known as the 'Boy Heroes'. U.S. forces occupy the capital

1848   War with the United States concludes with the signing of the Treaty of Guadalupe Hidalgo

1856   The Ley Lerdo strips the Catholic Church of privileges; many churches and monasteries in the capital are taken over by the authorities.

1857   On 5 February the Federal Constitution of the United Mexican States is signed. Mexico City becomes a Federal District

1864   The Austrian archduke Maximilian and his wife, Carlota, enter Mexico City after Maximilian is proclaimed Emperor of Mexico

1867   Maximilian is killed. The republic is restored

1877   Porfirio Díaz wins the presidency. He will dominate Mexico for more than three decades, and during this time he modernizes and expands the capital

1910   Celebrations commemorate the centenary of independence. The dictator Porfirio Díaz is deposed and the Mexican Revolution begins

1911   Francisco I. Madero is elected president in first free elections

1913   February sees the 'Tragic Ten Days', during which several hundred are killed in the uprising led by General Victoriano Huerta. President Madero is assassinated together with Vice President Pino Suárez. Huerta takes over the presidency

1917   A new national constitution is proclaimed. Venustiano Carranza becomes first president of the new republic

1920   Carranza is deposed by General Álvaro Obregón, who is elected president

1929   The National Revolutionary Party (later the PRI) is founded in Mexico City

1934   The Palacio de Bellas Artes is inaugurated more than twenty years after first being proposed

1946   The National Lottery building on the Paseo de la Reforma is completed

1950   The Viaducto Miguel Alemán is opened, signalling the start of massive infrastructure work in the capital

1968   On 2 October several hundred students are killed during a peaceful demonstration in the Plaza de las Tres Culturas, Tlatelolco. The Olympic Games open just ten days later on 12 October

1969   The first line of the French-built metro system opens

1985   A massive earthquake hits the centre of Mexico City, causing at least 10,000 deaths and leaving half a million people homeless

1997   The left-wing Andrés Manuel López Obrador becomes the first elected mayor of Mexico City

2000   Vicente Fox, of the right-wing National Action Party, takes over the presidency, becoming the first non-PRI president since Francisco I. Madero, nine decades earlier

2010   Commemoration of the bicentenary of independence from Spain

2017   Mexico's Federal District is officially renamed Ciudad de Mexico, or Mexico City, giving the local authorities greater autonomy

Suggested Reading and Viewing

Agustín, José, *Tragicomedia Mexicana* (Planeta, Mexico City, 1990)

Ayala Alonso, Enrique, *La casa de la ciudad de México* (Consejo Nacional para la Cultura y las Artes, Mexico City, 1996)

Baudot, Georges, *Utopia and History in Mexico: The First Chroniclers of Mexican Civilization* (Boulder, CO, 1995)

Blanco, José Joaquín, *Un chavo bien helado* (Mexico City, 1990)

—, *Ciudad de México. Espejos del siglo XX* (Mexico City, 2004)

Caistor, Nick, *Mexico City: A Cultural and Literary Companion* (Oxford, 2000)

Calderón de la Barca, Frances, *Life in Mexico* (Berkeley, CA, 1982)

Carrillo, Rafael A., *Posada and Mexican Engraving* (Mexico City, 1980)

Coe, Andrew, *Mexico City* (Hong Kong, 1994)

Constantine, Mildred, *Tina Modotti: A Fragile Life* (London, 1975)

Cortés, Hernán, *Letters from Mexico* (New Haven, CT, and London, 1986)

De Anda, Enrique, *Historia de la arquitectura Mexicana* (Barcelona, 2013)

Díaz del Castillo, Bernal, *The Discovery and Conquest of Mexico, 1517–1521* (New York, 1956)

Dugrand, Alain, *Trotsky in Mexico* (Manchester, 1992)

Enciclopedia de México, *Imagen de la gran capital* (Mexico City, 1985)

Fuentes, Carlos, *Aura* (New York, 1965)

—, *Where the Air is Clear* (New York, 1960)

Gage, Thomas, *The English American: A New Survey of the West Indies* (London, 1928)

Gallo, Rubén, ed., *The Mexico City Reader* (Madison, WI, 2004)

Gilbert, Alan, *The Latin American City* (London, 1997)

Greene, Graham, *The Lawless Roads* (London, 2002)

Herrera, Hayden, *Frida: A Biography of Frida Kahlo* (London, 1989)

Johns, Michael, *The City of Mexico in the Age of Díaz* (Austin, TX, 1997)

Kandell, Jonathan, *La Capital: The Biography of Mexico City* (New York, 1988)

Kerouac, Jack, *On the Road* (New York, 1960)

Krauze, Enrique, *Redeemers: Ideas and Power in Latin America,* (New York, 2012)

Krieger, Peter, ed., *Megalópolis* (Mexico City, 2006)

Lawrence, D. H., *The Plumed Serpent* (Harmondsworth, 1970)

Lewis, Oscar, *The Children of Sánchez* (New York, 1961)

—, *Five Families: Mexican Case Studies in the Culture of Poverty*
(New York, 1959)

Luiselli, Valeria, *The Story of my Teeth* (New York, 2016)

Marnham, Patrick, *So Far from God: A Journey to Central America*
(London, 1985)

Matos Moctezuma, Eduardo, *Vida y muerte en el Templo Mayor*
(Mexico City, 1994)

Monsiváis, Carlos, *Mexican Postcards* (London, 1997)

Newson, Linda A., and John P. King, *Mexico City through History and
Culture* (New York, 2009)

Poniatowska, Elena, *El último guajalote* (Mexico City, 1982)

—, *Massacre in Mexico* (New York, 1975)

Reed, John, *Insurgent Mexico* (New York, 1969)

Ross, John, *Mexico in Focus* (London, 1996)

Tenorio-Trillo, Mauricio, *I Speak of the City: Mexico City at the Turn
of the Twentieth Century* (Chicago, IL, 2012)

Terry, T. Philip, *Terry's Mexico* (London, 1911)

Thomas, Hugh, *The Conquest of Mexico* (London, 1993)

Tovar de Teresa, Guillermo, *La ciudad de los palacios* (Mexico City, 1992)

Valle Arizpe, Artemio de, *Historia de la Ciudad de México según los
relatos de sus cronistas* (Mexico City, 1997)

Villalobos, Juan Pablo, *I'll Sell You a Dog* (London, 2016)

Ward, Peter, *Mexico City* (London, 1990)

West, Rebecca, *Survivors in Mexico* (New Haven, CT, 2004)

Wolfe, Bertram D., *The Fabulous Life of Diego Rivera* (Chelsea, MI, 1990)

Blogs

'16 Quintessential Mexico City Experiences' www.sidetrackedtravelblog.com

'Best of Mexico City', www.gretastravels.com

'Mexico City: Three Day Itinerary', www.twowanderingsoles.com

'Mexico City in Three Days (or so)', www.lifeawesomeblog.com

'Mexico City Travel Guide', www.thetipsygypsies.net

Films

Amores perros, dir. Alejandro González Iñárritu (2000)
Attack dogs and violence in the slums of twenty-first-century
Mexico City

Cinco días sin Nora/Nora's Will, dir. Mariana Chenillo (2008)
Jewish life and death in the Mexican capital

Cronos, dir. Guillermo del Toro (1993)
Alchemy and horror in the film that launched Guillermo del Toro's
career

Días de gracia/Days of Grace, dir. Everardo Gout (2011)
Drugs, gangs and football in a paean to the Mexican capital

Frida, dir. Julie Taymor (2002)
Biopic of the iconic Mexican artist Frida Kahlo

Güeros, dir. Alonso Ruizpalacios (2014)
Coming-of-age drama depicting the lives of young university students
in the turbulent capital city

Los Olvidados/The Young and the Damned, dir. Luis Buñuel (1950)
The exiled Spanish director's classic account of forgotten street kids
in Mexico City

Spectre, dir. Sam Mendes (2015)
James Bond in action in the centre of the Mexican capital

Temporada de patos/Duck Season, dir. Fernando Eimbcke (2004)
Youthful angst in a Mexico City tower block

Acknowledgements

Many thanks to: Patricia and Valeria Arendar, Homero Aridjis, Roger Bartra, Christopher Domínguez Michel, Margo Glanz, Enrique Krauze, Carlos Monsiváis, Elena Poniatowska, Guillermo Sheridan and Juan Villoro, in Mexico City. In the UK: Adriana Díaz-Enciso, James Ferguson, Arlene Gregorius, John King and Jason Wilson. Also thanks to Vivian Constantinopoulos and the editors at Reaktion Books, plus the usual suspects: Amanda, Rachel, Ana and Lucia.

Photo Acknowledgements

The author and publishers wish to express their thanks to the below sources of illustrative material and/or permission to reproduce it.

Alamy Stock Photo: pp. 34 (Classic Image), 70 (The Granger Collection), 91 (Granger Historical Picture Archive, © Banco de México Diego Rivera Frida Kahlo Museums Trust, Mexico, D.F./DACS 2019); Valeria Arendar: pp. 125, 130, 182; p. 91; Nick Caistor: p. 133, 144; Centro de la Imagen: pp 65 (Antonio Reynoso), 110 (Hermanos Mayo), 112 and 114–15 (Enrique Bostelmann), 147 (Lourdes Grobet); Library of Congress, Washington, DC: pp. 23, 62, 63, 74, 75, 76, 77, 78, 88, 89, 92, 153; Sebastian Machado: pp. 14 bottom, 20, 184, 186, 187, 188, 189; Shutterstock: pp. 6, 156 and 157 (Anton_Ivanov), 7 (Bond RocketImages), 8 top (Diego Grandi), 8 bottom (Peter Zaharov), 9 (Marisol Rios Campuzano), 10 (Byelikova Oksana), 11 (Felix Lipov), 12 top (Dina Julayeva), 12 bottom (EddieHernandezPhotography), 13 top (Kamira), 13 bottom (Grigorev Mikhail), 14 top (Kartinkin77), 15 and 126 (Leonardo Design), 16 (ChameleonsEye), 21 (VictorMartinez), 30 (123455543), 68 (Diego Grandi), 72 (Inspired By Maps), 80 (Itzavᴜ), 102 (NadiyaRa), 105 (Kamira), 116, 120 (Ulrike Stein), 122 (BondRocketImages), 123 (carlos.araugo), 132 (Kit Leong), 134 (gary yim), 136 (ElHielo), 141 (Diego Grandi), 148 (bmszealand), 150 and 154–5 (Kamira), 160 (Aꜱ Food Studio), 167 (ChameleonsEye), 170 (schlyx), 171 and 172 (Quetzalcoatl1), 174 (Kiev.Victor), 177 (Chepe Nicoli), 178 (E Rojas), 191 (Nic Crilly-Hargrave).

Rosemania has published the image on p. 57 online, Matthew Rutledge has published the image on p. 106 online, ismael villafranco has published the image on p. 107 online, Rob Young has published the image on p. 142 online under conditions imposed by a Creative Commons Attribution Share Alike 2.0 Generic license; Daniel Case has published the image on pp. 119 and 139 online, Txtdgtl has published the image on p. 159 online, Thelmadatter has published the image on p. 164 online under conditions imposed by a Creative Commons Attribution Share Alike 3.0 Unported license; Thomas Ledl has published the image on p. 52 online,

Index

Page numbers in *italics* refer to illustrations